The RUTH STOUT
NO-WORK
Garden
BOOK

RUTH STOUT
&
RICHARD CLEMENCE

A RUTH STOUT CLASSICS *Collection*

Amaranth Leaves * Arrowroot * Artichoke * Arugula * Asparagus * Bamboo Shoots * Beans * Beets * Belgian Endive * Bitter Melon * Bok Choy * Broadbeans * Broccoli * Broccoli Rabe * Brussel Sprouts * Cabbage, Green * Cabbage, Red * Carrot * Cassava (Yuca Root) * Cauliflower * Celeriac (Celery Root) * Celery * Chayote * Chicory (Curly Endive) * Collards * Corn * Crookneck * Cucumber * Daikon * Dandelion Greens * Edamame * Eggplant * Fennel * Fiddleheads * Field Peas * Ginger Root * Horseradish * Jicama * Kale * Kohlrabi * Leeks * Lettuce, Iceberg * Lettuce, Leaf * Lettuce, Romaine * Mushrooms * Mustard Greens * Okra * Onion (Red) * Onions * Parsnip * Peas, Green * Pepper, Green * Red peppers * Pepper, Sweet Red * Potato, Red * Potato, White * Potato, Yellow * Pumpkin * Radicchio * Radishes * Rutabaga * Salsify (Oysterplant) * Shallots * Snow Peas * Sorrel * Spaghetti Squash * Spinach * Squash, Butternut * Sugar Snap Peas * Sweet Potato * Swiss Chard * Tomatillo * Tomato * Turnip * Watercress * Yam Root * Zucchini

"Why do people who like to get up early look with disdain on those who like to lie in bed late? And why do people who like to work feel superior to those who prefer to dream?"

Ruth Stout

NO-WORK *Garden* BOOK

RUTH STOUT
& RICHARD CLEMENCE

Cover Design by Andy Costabel of Costanera Creative. Find them at www.CostaneraCreative.com

Layout by Steven W. Siler

Photo editing by Beau Stevens
All photos common license unless otherwise noted.

To others unnamed, because my memory is as short as my hair.

You can find us at www.signaturetastes.com and on Facebook: Signature Tastes

To Stanley W. Siler
Who is a master of growing plants
and people...

Antique seed packets. Seed packets were designed to be small enough to be mailed in an envelope to customers, increasing their availability.

I have always wondered if anyone really reads the Table of Contents. Now since this book should be organized by proper headings such as Planting or Soil Preparation or the like. But let's be honest, that simply wouldn't be Ruth Stout's style.

Talking to plants to help them grow is a well-known old gardeners tale, but studies have shown vibration (like music, or perhaps even the sweet sound of your voice) can affect plant growth.

In ancient Egypt, onions were worshiped. People of ancient Egypt used to cover the tombs of their rulers with onion drawings, and onions played a vital role in burial rituals.

*W*hen Organic Gardening and Farming decided to publish, in book form, the articles that Richard Clemence and I had written for them through the years, they sent us the material to look over. To change, to improve, to correct? Well, in the second paragraph of the first article I wrote, I found something to change: that I freeze turnips, which I haven't done for years; I just leave them in the garden, cover them with bales of hay, and dig them, when wanted, all winter.

Realizing that these articles were full of reports of things about which I had later changed my mind, I decided that the sensible thing to do was not to alter anything. And why did I decide that? Perhaps because it would be too much work, but I rationalized my conclusion in this way: maybe it is more helpful to other gardeners to tell of the things

that seemed all right, but weren't, than to simply say "I do this, I do that".

So here is the story of the things I have learned, and "unlearned", about gardening. The first article was published in 1953, the last one in 1971. The later ones contain information which is contrary to some opinions and performances in my books on gardening.

Does it embarrass me to have to admit mistakes? No, it doesn't. "Nobody's perfect".

R.S.

Talking to plants to help them grow is a well-known old gardeners tale, but studies have shown vibration (like music, or perhaps even the sweet sound of your voice) can affect plant growth.

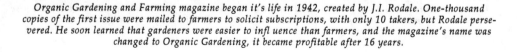

Organic Gardening and Farming magazine began it's life in 1942, created by J.I. Rodale. One-thousand copies of the first issue were mailed to farmers to solicit subscriptions, with only 10 takers, but Rodale persevered. He soon learned that gardeners were easier to infl uence than farmers, and the magazine's name was changed to Organic Gardening, it became profitable after 16 years.

A Note from the Editors

of

Organic Gardening and Farming

Magazine

To the editors and readers of OGF, Ruth Stout is special. Ever since she sent in her first article back in 1953, (which we promptly and unceremoniously lost), she has been a source of delight to everyone who has had a chance to ponder her nuggets of down-to-earth-common sense gardening wisdom. But more important than her "just plain folks" charm is the logical method of her year-round mulch system, a system that she has developed, perfected and reported in the pages of *Organic Gardening and Farming* magazine.

Ruth has maintained that most of the work associated with gardening—especially organic gardening— is unnecessary except for one thing: mulch. Permanent year-round mulch, in Ruth's eyes, is the permanent year-round answer to all the garden chores—and anything else you expend energy on is surplus effort or just "playing."

Needless to say, reaction to Ruth's deliberately controversial contentions is always expected—and always loud and emphatic. Thousands upon thousands of readers agree with her, generally with a word of thanks for her suggestions.

The ultimate goal of farming is not the growing of crops, but the cultivation and perfection of human beings.
Masanobu Fukuoka, The One-Straw Revolution

We've gotten more mail and more comments on her articles than on any others. Now our readers' service office braces for the wave when they learn that an article of hers is scheduled.

Here are some typical letters:

Dear Sir;

Orchids to Ruth Stout—mulched orchids! She is the greatest! I have tried to follow every word she has said since I first discovered her about 5 years ago. I'm for the "green thumb without the aching back" and her brand of hammock gardening. The best part of all is that it really works. I have been receiving free loads of leaves from the city each fall. Last year, which was the driest in 80 years, the squash grew beautifully without a drop of water. The more leaves, the better. Nor have I used any poisons on the garden for the past 5 years.

This year a neighbor has allowed me the use of her vacant lot and the city dumped about 15 loads of leaves there last fall. So I plan to expand and try several other of Ruth Stout's ideas.

Oh yes, lots of birds have arrived since I quit using poisons and set up a birdbath for them. They take care of all the bugs and save all that work on my part.

RALPH F. SPITZER
Helena, Montana

Dear Sir:

As one journalist to another I want to compliment J. I. Rodale and his staff for publishing one of the finest agricultural magazines

"The central paradox and challenge of marriage is that we have to make family out of someone we're not related to..."

— Ruth Stout

that crosses my desk. The format, writing, photography and artwork of *Organic Gardening* are all superb. What I especially enjoy is the editorial each month. With a very limited background in agriculture, I find ,your editorials very enlightening.

I think your January issue was especially well done. The cover photo of Ruth Stout, beaming with pride in her garden, is a journalism classic. Mrs. Stout's story with accompanying illustrations was delightful and fascinating. The story is going into my keep-forever file. If I ever get the urge to till the soil, I will use her story as a beginning.

Congratulations for your contribution to U.S. agriculture.

TOM CAHILL
Editor, *Seedmen's Digest*
San Antonio, Texas

Dear Sir:

I shall not try to identify myself at length. Suffice to say that I have twice inspected Ruth's garden and grounds with envy and have written to her several times for advice. I greatly admire her horticultural prowess, her wit and her flawless rhetoric (to use that currently much abused word).

Now I write to thank you for your "Why? And Why Not?" article in *Organic Gardening* magazine. After reading for many years of the mammoth, bug-free, luxuriant, etc., etc., some of them brand new, I am beholden to Ruth for admitting that all is not pure perfection even in an organic garden. I have had this North Carolina garden

Farmers are philosophical. They have learned that it is less wearing to shrug than to beat their breasts."

— Ruth Stout

(about the size of yours) for seven years. I couldn't count the bales of hay, bushels of leaves, weeds and grass clippings which have served as mulch, following her admirable directives. The soil is beautiful beyond belief. Nevertheless I suffer some crushing and inexplicable defeats. This year green peppers and eggplant were virtual nothings. Cabbage last spring was a disappointment. Conversely tomatoes, zucchini, beans and squash were outstanding.

Thank you again for sharing some failures with the readers of Mr. Rodale's publication.

THEODOSA MARTIN
Tryon, North Carolina

But let's be completely honest. Some readers don't see Ruth's year-round mulch method as the complete answer to gardening bonanzas. The sharp-penned Queen of Mulch asserts in blunt, bold terms that no gardener need ever bother with making compost, digging soil or using power equipment. Them's fighting words to most organic gardeners!

Dorothy Schroeder, a long-time contributor to OGF, may have summarized their objections:

"Keep your garden under wraps, covered by a deep porous mulch for soil enrichment, climate and moisture control, increased humus, and a minimum of insect damage." The paraphrase is mine, but the thought is Ruth Stout's, and a truer thought was never expressed. So far I am entirely in agreement with Ruth's method. But she goes on to say that this mulch is all that is necessary for the gar-

"When we contemplate buying something, we usually ask the price of it, then decide whether or not it is worth that much to us. But when we expend time and energy, we often just go ahead and pay."

— *Ruth Stout*

den—and there she and I part company.

"I'd like to say at the outset that Ruth Stout has given me many of the garden practices that make my garden the joy to me that it is. My garden has been covered with mulch since Ruth first advocated it, many years ago. That was a different garden from the one I have now, but so successful that I gratefully brought my Ruth-acquired knowledge to my new garden.

"Ruth Stout taught me to solve the backbreaking job of removing old roots and weeds by covering them with so many layers of newspaper that they simply died beneath the weight of public opinion, thus replacing age-old weeds with the decaying vegetation that my garden woefully lacked.

"Because of Ruth Stout's teaching, my new asparagus bed was a dalliance, not an engineering project. It is better than the old one.

"There is no argument about production, either. You can double the tomato harvest, triple the corn, and do even better with lettuce and radishes, all with mulch. Everything I've tried growing under it has prospered. But for my garden—and I believe for many others— it is necessary to take that step further, and compost.

"When my corn droops and hangs limply on a hot day, the thing to think is that it is thirsty, and to give it water. But it reacts in exactly the same way if the soil is waterlogged and air isn't able to reach the roots. Given a heavy rain or the hose injudiciously left on the corn patch, mulch would do nothing to cure this condition, but compost in the soil would sponge up the surplus water, and feed it to the corn as it became necessary.

"I love spring anywhere, but if I could choose I would always greet in a garden."

— Ruth Stout

"Then there are the plants that have the wrong pH for their development. They show, for example, a nitrogen lack in their leaves when there is plenty of nitrogen in the soil. It is unavailable to the hungry plants because, since the soil is too acid, the manganese in it is insoluble, and since manganese is necessary to make the nitrogen available—no nitrogen! Over and over this frustrating problem is encountered. You have all the symptoms of a deficiency of something necessary to the development of a plant, and the culprit is the acid-alkaline balance. What to do? Go to the heart of the problem and correct the balance. How? With compost in the soil.

"You can, of course, add limestone to an acid soil; cottonseed meal and acid peat to an alkaline. But you must consider that you may have plants that need acidity growing next to ones that need their soil on the alkaline side. Potatoes like their soil quite acid; asparagus, beets, peas and apples like theirs about neutral. You have only one garden, just a few feet or yards to grow all of these. The answer is humus in the soil, not just over it. Compost stores the minerals necessary to the plants and feeds them, along with stored water, as they need them to the roots.

"I admit that, given time, Ruth's mulch would provide that humus to the soil. In my very alkaline Colorado soil and with my low rainfall, it would take, I fear, a very long time. The fact that my soil was so alkaline when I took it over, after generations of gardening, in itself shows how little could be done.

"Ruth has arrived where I am going. She has achieved what I would like to have. Her garden is rich in the minerals mine all too

Cauliflowers grow so fast that sometimes you can hear the florets rubbing together. This sound is known as 'cauliflower creak.'

woefully lacks. They are available to her plants. I'm going in her direction, following, to a great extent, her pointing finger. But I don't have too many years to attain my goal. I, too, am an aging female, seeking health with the glorious annual rebirth that only a gardener knows. My garden still has to become self-sufficient, replacing what is taken from it. It is doing a good job, but it must do better. Health must be reaped from the garden rows. For that, considering my time limitations, I must have compost."

You can bet that those luke-warm advocates of the year-round mulch method would get a pointed rebuttal to their reservations — (she has a way of getting the last word!) But rather than stir up more heated controversy, let's let her talk in her own behalf. She's been doing all right like that for a long time!

—The Editors

In ancient Rome, one of the most common cooking ingredients was called "laser", from the silphium plant. It does not exist today. It was so delicious that it was harvested to extinction from its natural habitat in what is now Libya. We think that it probably tasted something like garlic.

Tomatoes were put "on trial" on June 28, 1820, in Salem, New Jersey. In front of a courthouse, Robert Johnson ate tomatoes in order to prove they weren't poisonous. The crowd waited for him to die but he didn't. Before that everyone in America used to think tomatoes were poisonous, due to them being a member of the nightshade family.

CHAPTER 1.

Throw Away Your Spade and Hoe!

WHEN SOMEONE, NOT LONG AGO, saw my garden for the first time and heard the method I've worked out, she exclaimed: "Why, you can grow vegetables until you're a hundred! From a wheelchair, if necessary."

I'm not a particularly vigorous woman, but I do all the work in a garden 40 by 60 feet, raising enough vegetables for my husband, my sister, myself and many guests. I freeze every variety, from early asparagus to late turnips. We never buy a vegetable.

I also do my housework, raise quite a few flowers, rarely do any work after 1 p.m. I'm scarcely ever more than just pleasantly tired. Dinner at night usually requires about half an hour's time, with food from a deep freeze to rely on.

Now I'm not boasting, at least not about what a whiz of an or-

"The longer I live the greater is my respect for manure in all its forms."
- Elizabeth von Arnim

ganizer, or something, I am. But I am proud of having figured out a way of gardening which brings top results with a minimum of labor. Would you, perhaps, wish to be able to garden until you're really getting along? Well, you can.

Many years ago, my husband and I moved from New York City to a farm in Connecticut, and I could hardly wait to plant a garden. We had a much too large plot plowed up, and that first summer I struggled with stones and fresh sod in which the spot abounded. And I of course hoed, weeded, and cultivated.

For several summers thereafter, I kept growing more than we could use, foolishly unwilling not to utilize the whole plot, since I had spent so much time getting it in shape. But gradually I did reduce the size of my garden, until, some time ago, it was only a third as large as it was originally. However, it was still too much work; I, of course, wasn't quite as full of pep as I had been, and also I was now trying to can all the surplus.

The only jobs in the garden I didn't do were the plowing and harrowing; every other thing I had always done myself. And very eager as I was each spring to get started, it seemed that usually everyone had just broken or loaned his plow, or had had some other calamity, when I was rarin' to put in some peas.

About twenty years ago, I was as usual trying to be patient until someone could do some plowing for me, when finally, one day, I used my head. No, not for plowing—for reasoning. My asparagus was doing beautifully and I said to myself: that ground hasn't been plowed for over ten years; what has asparagus got that peas haven't?

Colorful blooms aren't the chief reason these insects love your garden – it's more about the fragrance and nectar. According to the Smithsonian Institute, new cultivars of popular flowers have been bred for enhanced color and size, but have often lost their fragrance in the process. So everyday weeds, like dandelions and clovers, might actually be the most appealing things in your yard to butterflies (they hate pesticides, too).

To heck with plowing! I'm going to plant.

So, a little fearfully, I started to put in peas and spinach, intending to dig a minor trench first to loosen the earth. But I found that the mulch (leaves and hay) which I had dumped on the garden in the fall (to be plowed under in the spring) had kept the earth soft and moist; I merely needed to clear a spot with the rake and drop the seeds.

And having once started to take things into my own hands, I kept on. If I scramble around and get lots of mulch, I thought, and completely cover the garden with it (six or eight inches thick), no weeds can get through and the sun can't bake the soil. Even by the end of June, when I plant the last corn and the second beets, carrots, and so on, the ground will surely still be soft. And it was—but I'm getting ahead of myself.

Our milkman, a farmer, was glad to give me what he called "spoiled hay" and I called wonderful mulch. I spread it thickly over the entire garden, except, of course, on top of the seeds I had just planted. I did, however, put a lot over the asparagus, as I knew that could come up through the mulch. In a couple of years I abandoned all commercial fertilizers.

After putting the hay around, I soon found that the only jobs left were planting, thinning, and the picking. Whenever I wanted to put in some seeds, I raked the mulch back and planted, and later, when the seeds had sprouted, I pulled the mulch close around the little plants, thus keeping the ground around them moist, and outwitting the weeds.

A sunflower is not just one flower. Both the fuzzy brown center and the classic yellow petals are actually 1,000 – 2,000 individual flowers, held together on a single stalk.

Naturally the neighboring farmers at first laughed at me; for a few years they doted on stopping in in the spring to ask if I didn't want some plowing done. But, little by little, they were impressed by my results, and when they finally had to admit that the constantly rotting mulch of leaves and hay was marvelously enriching my soil, they didn't tease anymore. On the contrary, they would stop by to "have one more look" before finally deciding to give up plowing and spading and to mulch their own gardens.

My plot has become so rich that I can plant very closely, and I don't even use manure now. The garden is one-eighth its original size and so luxuriant that in the fall we call it the jungle; one of my carrots, sweet and tender, was large enough to serve five people. My sweet Spanish onions average a pound apiece; some weigh a pound and a quarter.

I have never liked to transplant (it would be impractical, anyway, from that wheel chair of the future), so I plant such things as cabbage, cauliflower, and so forth, twelve or fifteen inches apart and then pull out all but one in each group.

Another item: do you have trouble with bush peas bending over — lying on the ground and rotting in wet weather? All you need do is pull an extra amount of hay up to them on all sides and they stand as straight as tin soldiers, no matter how loaded with peas they are. And they are easy to pick.

I mulch the flowers too, but, I use the leaves and hay from the vegetable garden after it has rotted sufficiently to look almost like earth. Sweet peas, which seem to be difficult to grow here about, re-

There are more microorganisms in one teaspoon of soil than there are people on earth. It's aliiiiive! Mwahhha-hah, ok in all seriousness, that fact might make you uncomfortable, but microbes are important for keeping your soil full of nutrients.

spond miraculously to my system; I don't dig a trench, use no manure, but plant them in the vegetable garden and mulch them. This past dry summer, when even some artesian wells in our locality gave out, didn't faze my sweet peas. I've never had more, or nicer ones, didn't water them at all, and picked the last lot in mid-September. There is much talk nowadays of compost piles, and they are fine, but hard and cumbersome work for a woman.

I haven't used any kind of poison for bugs for years and I never see a bean beetle, a corn borer, aphis, or cutworm. I stopped using poisons simply because I hated the thought of them, and at first I couldn't understand why the bugs didn't plague me. Was a kind Providence rewarding me for—well, I didn't know what for, or were these tales I had heard lately about organic gardening really true? I didn't feel that I knew enough about the subject to argue the point, so I settled for being grateful that some little fairy, organic or otherwise, was keeping the pests out of my garden.

If you have to garden and are not very enthusiastic about it, it seems to me my method is your answer; you can do the job with a minimum of time and labor. And if, as I do, you love such work, it is also the answer; you can keep at it indefinitely.

So hunt up a second-hand store and get rid of your hoes and spades and cultivator; the largest digging tool you will need is a trowel. And when, although you're really getting along in years, you have a wonderful garden, and people marvel and ask who does the heavy work, you can truthfully reply: "There is no heavy work."

Some of your favorite fruits are actually in the rose family. Apples, peaches, and pears -oh my! Plus cherries, raspberries, strawberries, and more are rosaceae, making them realtives to the long-stemmed Valentine's Day variety.

THE QUESTIONS PEOPLE ASK

Visitors to my garden invariably ask a lot of questions. That's understandable, I guess, since long ago I discarded any ideas to plow, spade, harrow, sow a cover crop, hoe, cultivate, weed, water, spray, or build a compost pile. I simply keep everything under a year- round mulch.

One question is often repeated: *How much mulch is needed to start out with the 8-inch thickness which I strongly advocate?* I can't answer that because I gardened in this way long before I ever thought of writing about it, so I didn't keep track of any details. However, Richard Clemence says he thinks that 25 bales of hay at 50 pounds each would be about the minimum for an area of 50 feet by 50 feet, or about a half ton of loose hay.

Many people don't realize that in a mulched garden the seeds are planted in the earth in the usual way; you push back the mulch from a spot, put the seeds in the ground, and when they germinate you pull the mulch back up close to, and around, the tiny plants. A plant ing of small seeds should be left uncovered, although you can, if you wish to, sprinkle some sawdust on them, or cover the seeds with a little loose, coarse hay. They will come up through both these coverings, something I could hardly believe when told, but I tried it and find that it works.

Large seeds, however, such as corn, peas, beans or squash, may be covered immediately after planting with a few inches of loose hay. This keeps the weeds down, holds in moisture, and, in the case

The right orchid combination can smell like your favorite dessert. Delicious, so did you know that the vanilla bean comes from a orchid varietal? And it's not the only sweet-smelling kind: "An oncidum hyrbrid called Sharry Baby smells like chocolate," says George Hatfield, president of the Santa Barbara Orchid Show. "It's 'baking cookie' aroma has made it a winner."

of corn, stumps the crows.

I am asked over and over *why isnt it bad to mulch with hay which is full of weed seeds?* Well, if the mulch is thick enough, the weeds can't come through. When I say this, people then invariably ask why it is that the vegetable seeds come through and weed seeds don't; this is because heavy mulch is on top of the latter, but not the former. As I said above, a planting of small seeds shouldn't be covered with mulch, or at the most a narrow board, strip of paper or half-inch of sawdust will keep the ground soft and moist.

How can you safely plant tiny seeds between 8-inch walls of mulch? The answer is that almost before one gets through spreading it, the mulch begins to settle and soon becomes a two-or-three-inch compact mass, rather than an 8-inch fluffy one. It will no doubt be walked on, and rain may come; in any case it will settle, and you won't need 8 inches to start if you use solid chunks of baled hay.
Many people want to know why I don't use manure, and what 1 have against it. I have nothing against it; in fact I have a somewhat exaggerated respect for it. But I no longer need it; the ever-rotting mulch all over my plot takes its place.

I have been asked many times *should such things as sawdust and oak leaves be avoided,* the idea being that they make soil too acid. I can't answer this from very much experience, but I have had reports from many gardeners to the effect that they have used both sawdust and oak leaves over their entire gardens with satisfac tory results.

People want to know *what to use for mulch*. Well, hay, straw, leaves, pine needles, sawdust, weeds, garbage—any vegetable matter that rots.

Don't some leaves decay too slowly? No, they just remain mulch longer, which cuts down labor. Don't they mat down? If so, it doesn't matter, since they are between the rows of growing things, not on top of them. Can one use leaves without hay? Yes, but a combination of the two is better, I think.

Shouldn't the hay be chopped? Don't you have a terrible time spreading long hay? Well, I don't have mine chopped and I don't have a terrible time, and I'm 86 and no stronger than the average.

Can you use grass clippings? Yes, but unless you have a huge lawn, they don't go very far. Anyway, although I don't know much about it, I believe it is supposed to be good for the lawn to leave the grass on it where it falls as it is cut.

How often do you put on mulch? Whenever you see a spot that needs it. If weeds begin to peep through anywhere, just toss an armful of hay on them.

What time of year do you start to mulch? The answer is now, whatever the date may be; at least begin to gather your material. Or at the very least give the matter constructive thought at once; make plans. If you are intending to use only leaves, you will unfortunately have to wait until they fall off the trees, but you can be prepared to make use of them the moment they drop.

Many ask; ***Shall I spread manure and plow it under and then mulch?*** Yes, if your soil isn't very rich: otherwise, mulch alone will answer the purpose.

When shall I put on lime, and how much, and should it be put on top

Archaeologists have uncovered evidence that grapes were grown to make wine about 8,000 years ago in Mesopotamia (today's Iraq), although the ancient Egyptians were the first to record the process of making wine about 5,000 years ago.

of the hay or under it? Of the three questions here, the first two have nothing to do with mulching. You proceed with the addition of lime just as you did before you ever heard of my system of mulching; you can have your soil tested through your agricultural agent, I have, however, heard it said (and not by a fanatic) that my way of gardening may automatically take care of the problem of an acid soil; the idea seems to be that before long a mulched garden teems with earthworms and these little helpers tend to make earth alkaline.

As to the third question about lime, you can put it either right in the dirt as you plant, or on top of the mulch, providing you add it at a time of year when you can reasonably expect rain or snow to wash it through the mulch by the time the soil should have it. I haven't used any lime for five years and things are doing all right.

How far apart should the rows be? The same distance they should be if you weren't mulching. After you have mulched for a few years, however, your soil will become so rich from rotting vegetable matter that you can plant much more closely than you would dare to if gardening the old-fashioned way. I am also strongly in favor of Richard Clemence's way of planting in rows a foot or two wide.

Doesn't a lot of mulch on flower beds make mounds of them? No, it doesn't, but don't ask me why; I only know that my heavily mulched beds are even with the lawn.

Doesn't mulching look awful? Well, there are a lot of answers to that, and they depend largely on the mulcher; that is, how much he cares about having it look attractive. It doesn't have to look bad. And, I could come back with another question: Doesn't a sun baked or

Per kilogram, in the USA, asparagus has a larger carbon footprint than pork or veal. This is because of carbon emissions from transportation. Much of asparagus in the USA comes from Peru.

weedy garden look awful?

Doesn't mulch attract slugs, since the earth under it is always moist? I never thought so (I have no slugs), but I didn't know how to answer this question until I read what the *Encyclopedia of Organic Gardening* has to say about it: that a well-mulched garden, after there is plenty of humus in the soil, attracts earthworms and that tends to make the soil alkaline which slugs don't like. Isn't that a break? If slugs are really a problem, try the beer treatment described in the section "Garden Pests—They Aren't So Bad!"

How long does the mulch last? That depends on the kind you use. Try always to have some in reserve, so that it can be replenished as needed.

Where does one get mulch? Well, if enough people in a community demand it, I think someone will be eager to supply it. You probably know quite a few others who garden and who would be glad to join in the project. Use all the leaves around and the tops of perennials; clip your own corn stalks into foot-length pieces and use them. Utilize your garbage—any and all vegetable matter that rots.

As to spoiled hay, (hay that for some reason or other isn't good enough to feed to livestock; it may, for instance, have become moldy if it was moist when put in the haymow), it is just as effective and satisfactory for mulch as good hay, and a great deal cheaper.

In many localities the utility companies grind up the branches which they cut off when clearing wires, and they are often glad to dump them near your garden without charge. But hurry up before the companies find out that there is a demand for them, and decide to

---

The word pineapple comes from European explorers who thought the fruit combined the look of a pinecone with flesh like that of an apple. Pineapples are the only edible members of the bromeliad family.

make a fast buck. These wood chips make a splendid mulch, and I suggest you just ignore anyone who tells you they are too acid.

And I ignore the remarks (which are, however, extremely rare) belittling year-round, undisturbed mulch. If anyone, after taking a look at my flourishing garden, can think up ways to better it, let him do so, by all means. But if his "improvements" call for sprays, fertilizers, compost piles and labor, he needn't expect me to adopt them.

WHY? (AND WHY NOT?)

Sometimes, when you're bored and can't seem to think of any pleasing or constructive way of filling an hour or two, see if you can come up with some answers to the reasons why growing plants (and those which refuse to grow) behave in such various ways at differ ent times. And if you're the sort of person who comes to conclusions promptly — even though they are more or less based on questionable and unreliable premises — my guess is that quite a few of your answers will prove to be untenable.

Here are various happenings in my years of gardening — and I defy anyone to come up with answers to them, which carry any conviction! As a matter of fact, really knowledgeable people don't even attempt to explain the caprices of plants, and here's an example of this: When my first book about mulching was published, gardeners began to come and have a look at a vegetable patch which hadn't been plowed for 11 years. And it so happened that that summer, although my pepper plants were unusually large and healthy-looking,

---

Did you know... From a botanical standpoint, avocados and pumpkins are fruits, not vegetables, because they bear the plants' seeds. Rhubarb, on the other hand, is a vegetable.

not one pepper showed up. I had heard that if some plants are overnourished, they don't bloom or bear fruit, and I thought that this might be the answer to my pepper situation. But I began to doubt that theory when every one of the gardeners with whom I came in contact at that time was having the same trouble— no peppers on his plants. So I wrote to Carl Warren of Joseph Harris & Co., who had been of tremendous help to me through the years, asking him "how come," and he replied: "That's the way peppers are behaving this year." He'd had so much experience with plants that he had long since realized that there are some things which no one can figure out.

A few remarks about asparagus. Although "authorities" have stopped insisting that one dig a very deep trench for the roots, they are still saying that a hole eight inches deep is essential, and of course still giving other instructions about growing asparagus, fertilizing it, and so on. Since I long ago lost faith in so-called experts, I bought two dozen asparagus roots a few years ago and decided to try planting them by just laying them on top of the ground (in a bed of peonies) and tossing hay on them. And I have had a fine crop from these roots every season. You see, I had noticed that in a dozen or more places— in the meadow, by the woodshed, and around—asparagus plants were showing up. Obviously, birds or wind had scattered the seeds, and some of these "wild" plants are more luxurious than those in my regular asparagus bed. One volunteer in particular, which has been producing for years, is about three times as big as any other I've seen anywhere. And of course it gets no fertilization and no weeding around it; in fact, the grass grows right up against it. In regard to vol-

Where did Poinsettias originate from? Well they were natives of Mexico, were brought to the United States in 1825 by the first U.S. minister to Mexico, Joel Poinsett, for whom the plant is named.

unteer plants — and although my garden is completely and carefully mulched — a few tomatoes pop up here and there in my plot each season. These get a later start of course than the plants I set out, but they all produce fruit at about the same time. And the volunteers seem to be more prolific. (I always buy tomato plants — never grow them from seeds.)

BUTTERCUP squash is at the head of the class around here. I've planted it along with a few other kinds for years. And planted just about tells the whole story as far as our favorite is concerned, for the vines have scarcely ever produced more than one or two very small squash. However, last summer buttercup out did all the other varieties, and the jumper-to-conclusions might say: "That was because of so much rain." But I can't accept this, because buttercup did almost as well the year before, when we had practically no rain. As for blue hubbard, the largest one in this past rainy season weighed only ten pounds, while my vines produced a 51-pound blue hubbard some years ago in a very dry year.

Several years ago I planted Chinese cabbage and kale — rather late, as always — and the latter was a complete flop. But the cabbages grew to be very large; one of the heads weighed seven pounds. Last season the cabbage did very badly, however, hardly making any solid center at all, while the kale was practically sensational. I planted quite a lot of it because to me it's nice to have a few vegetables that will stay on in the garden until Christmas. There was so much kale out there that I had to look around to find people who like it to take some.

Why to cranberries float? Small pockets of air inside cranberries cause them to bounce and float in water.

If I hadn't really given up on trying to find answers to the vagaries of plants, I might conclude that the vines of the buttercup squash, which wandered over half of my plot last summer, had overwhelmed the Chinese cabbage. And speaking of cabbage, the early variety of the other kind came through very well for me, while the late type did almost nothing.

Out of my six plants of broccoli, both early and late, only one produced, and the same was true of purple cauliflower. The fruit that did materialize however was in both cases, unusually large and fine. When a whole crop gives up—as that late cabbage did—one feels sure there must be a good reason, even though obscure. But when several plants, growing side by side, behave completely differently, it sure is baffling, as, for instance, going out to your patch after a cold night to find that one of two plants, which are only an inch or two apart, is frozen and the other in good condition.

Last year I planted turnips in the same spot where they had done very well the preceding season, and they gave up almost before they got a start. So again the inveterate conclusion-jumper says: "Sure. You should rotate crops." But I also planted this vegetable that same day in another part of the garden where it had also been grown the year before, and these latter tur nips couldn't have done better. They were huge. Any questions? Or, more to the point, any answers?

Of course a gardener can't help wondering why this and why that—but even if one comes up with some sort of answer now and then, it does seem wiser not to broadcast it!

THE COUCH I GARDEN ON

Peanuts start out as flowers above ground. They then wilt, and the remaining peg goes back into the ground and turns into a peanut.

When I tell someone that I do all of the work in my vegetable garden, besides several flower beds, someone invariably asks: "What time do you get up?" The answer to that, at any time of year, is: when I feel like it. When gardeners who aren't letting mulch do most of their work are weeding, hoeing, watering and maybe indulging in a bit of swearing at times—we mulchers can do just about as "the spirit moves us"—be outside if that's our desire, but stay inside if the sun is too hot, etc. And our plants won't suffer from lack of attention.

When you plant in a garden which is already mulched, first mark the row, then pull the hay away from that spot and plant right in the earth, just as you would if you were gardening the old-fashioned way.

Onion sets may just be scattered around on last year's mulch, then covered with a few inches of loose hay; by this method you can "plant" a pound of them in a few minutes, and you may do it, if you like, before the ground thaws. Also, lettuce seeds will germinate if merely thrown on frozen earth—but not on top of mulch. And this, of course, can't be done if you plow before planting.

Many people have discovered that they can lay seed potatoes on last year's mulch, or on the ground or even on sod, cover them with about a foot of loose hay, and later simply pull back the mulch and pick up the new potatoes. In case you haven't noticed, potato plants and their flowers are quite pretty, so you can start this crop in a flower bed if you like. Ours is placed at one end of the bed of iris.

A few weeds may come through your mulch here and there;

In 1986 a California farmer named Mike Yurosek was unhappy that he was unable to sell his imperfect carrots. So he cut and shaved them into cuter versions and called them "baby-cut" carrots. Before the invention of the baby carrot, each American ate 6 lbs of carrot a year, now they eat 11 lbs a year.

this will be because you didn't apply it thickly enough to defeat them. They are easy to pull if you want to take the trouble, but the simplest thing is to just toss a bit of hay on top of them. And if a row of something such as turnips or carrots needs thinning, this can be done effectively by simply covering the plants you want to get rid of with a httle mulch.

My garden chores in the fall are much the same as in summer—harvesting and freezing the produce. About the middle of November I spread hay around and rake leaves. Now is also a good time to carry some hay into the corn patch with a pitchfork, putting chunks all along the rows. Next spring, I will prop up my pea plants with it when this vegetable is planted between the rows of corn. And I can take anywhere from a week to a month for this hay job; there's no reason for it to make me feel pushed. I'll put a few bales on top of the row of carrots, and will dig them throughout the winter, whenever I want some.

And speaking of winter—well, if I'm writing a book, I spend most of the morning at it (on the couch, where else?), but with my conviction that exercise is one of the 4 major ingredients for good health, I see to it that I get it. A sort of basic house-cleaning is helpful here. And outdoors, these past few months before the snow interfered, I chopped down quite a few trees—not exactly giant redwoods, but not saplings, either! After the snow came and stayed, I shoveled a path to the woodshed. Out there, protected from the wind and with the warm sun cooperating. I've been doing some wood-chopping each day, for my health and pleasure —and, oh yes, for the fireplace,

Cockroaches won't eat cucumbers. This is due to a chemical in cucumbers (trans-2-nonenal) which acts as a natural repellent for ants and roaches.

too.

I order my seeds and arrange the packets alphabetically, make a diagram for the coming season's planting, and write a weekly column—all of which can be termed "work," so I do it in the morning, knocking off at one o'clock. However, since my first garden book was published, thousands of people have called here, morning, afternoon or evening, to have a first-hand look at my mulch system. But showing them around and answering their questions isn't "work," really.

About the hardest work is probably making up your mind to one thing: If you are the only person in your neighborhood who is using this no-plow, no-spade, no- cultivating method, your friends and neighbors will say you are crazy. Ignore them. They will change their tune.

MAKE MINE MORE MULCH!

When someone suggested, not long ago, that I write in reply to the arguments against a year-round mulch, my first reaction was to ask myself why I should argue with people who don't know the score. For my conviction is that any gardener who hasn't given this method at least a 3-year chance to prove itself has hardly any basis for opposition to it. And if he has mulched for that long a time, he will be sold on the idea!

Why do I say three years? Well, any grower knows that no plants behave exactly the same every year. But if something should go wrong when you first begin the mulching method, you may be in-

---

Raisa Gorbachev once told a British minister there were more than 300 ways to cook potatoes in the USSR. When he had doubts, she sent him a cookbook and a note saying, "My apologies for being somewhat inaccurate: in fact, there are five hundred, rather than three hundred, recipes to cook potatoes."

clined to put the blame where it doesn't belong. If, for instance, your mulch is too skimpy and some weeds come through it, you'll feel the idea doesn't work. And if slugs show up, you'll say this is no doubt because of the hay and leaves on your patch. I've mulched for many years—and have no slugs in my garden. If you do, set shallow containers of beer out in your patch for them, and they will die happy. (I've been told that slugs go for beer but that it "does them in," so to speak!)

If you have a clay-ey soil, you will probably need to mulch your garden for several years before getting to the point where you can relax. My soil is sandy, so I have to rely on what I've been told about how to solve this problem, which is to dig in plenty of good material such as hay, corncobs, leaves, weeds, etc., to lighten the dirt. (Not peat moss, though, for the scientists say that it has no nutritive value, and in this instance I go along with them.) If you do this for two or three seasons, you can then mulch your patch and take it easy.

The diehards love to declare that soil covered with hay warms up more slowly than it would if left bare. And they insist that this causes big problems when you try to plant early crops. Well, no doubt any 10-year-old could come up with the answer to this, which is to decide in the fall where you want to put early crops, pull the hay off those spots, then put the mulch back in the spring. And even if you don't do this, you are able, in my experience, to plant earlier than you could if you have to plow first.

Another "old wives' tale" is that plants which are mulched will freeze more readily than unmulched ones. That I don't believe. When

Wales' national symbol is a leek because, on the eve of the battle against the Saxons, St. David advised the Britons to wear leeks in their caps so as to easily distinguish friend from foe. This helped to secure a great victory.

I first heard this complaint, I experimented for several seasons by pushing the hay away from some plants, and it turned out that they were no safer than the others. In this connection, mulch-detractors also declare that asparagus is delayed by mulching, and since it is one of the very early crops, gardeners are eager for it to mature. Well, number one, if asparagus comes too early, it is likely to get frozen before you pick it; and number two, it's not much of a job to pull the mulch to one side and let the ground thaw. Best of all, since this vegetable is a 6-week crop and you may wish it lasted longer, why not push the mulch back on half of the bed and leave it on the rest, thereby getting an 8-week stretch?

One professor of agriculture, who was against year- round mulch, went on at great length about the terrible time growers using it have with frost. He advised us to stay up and spray our plants with water all night in freezing weather. Well, if this man had what it takes to put prejudice aside and really give mulching a try, he would find that on cold nights all he would need to do (and in an unbelievably short time) would be to toss the hay — lying there handy — onto his plants. Then the professor could calmly go to bed, and happily dream that he was a reasonable human being who tried out a thing before he damned it.

Every now and then I hear that gardeners who are willing to keep a constant mulch on all other plants are, strangely enough, afraid to mulch their corn. I wish I knew why they feel this way. All I can do to assure them is to report that for 25 years I've had a constant mulch in my corn belt — and of course I do no digging or hoeing or

Sulfuric compounds are to blame for cut onions bringing tears to your eyes. According to the National Onion Association, chilling the onion and cutting the root end last reduces the problem.

weeding or watering or fertilizing. As for that last term, I do take care always to use old hay, which is beginning to rot, for the corn rows — between them, that is, and around the stalks. Also, the pea vines, which I've planted between the rows of corn, are left there to die and become mulch, and the old soybean plants are disposed of in the same way. My rows of corn are two feet apart and the plants are spaced to 8 inches. There are two good ears on just about every stalk, and when the second ear has been picked, I clip off the stalk and leave it lying there in the patch. The reason I don't remove the roots is because they can be used the next season for a guide in planting; this eliminates using a string to make straight rows.

In case anyone might wonder why the peas (LINCOLN, of course, from Joseph Harris) don't fall over the cornstalks, the reason is because the hay props them up — which makes them easy to pick and keeps them dry. And I use the same idea for tomatoes, planting them along the fence (which entirely surrounds the garden) and putting big gobs of hay against them, causing them to lean against the fence. It doesn't really call for any extra work, for the hay will be used for the fall mulching.

Vaguely, I can understand the attitude of the old dyed-in-the-wool farmer who bypasses both mulching and compost piles. He's in a rut — and, by gum, he's going to stay there! But as for the more up-to-date gardener, who may do year-round mulching, but who also bothers with a compost pile, here's a bit of unasked- for advice: Better see a psychiatrist. One argument that's used against mulching flower beds is that the effect is unattractive, but I happen to think that hay is

Peanuts are not nuts, but legumes related to beans and lentils. They have more protein, niacin, folate, and phytosterols than any nut, according to the National Peanut Board,

as pleasing to the eye as dirt is. And I feel fairly sure that if people had been exposed to mulched flowers all of their lives, they would prefer the beds that way. Also, if some "queer" person tried to convince them that bare soil around flowers was more to be desired than hay or leaves, I doubt if they would go along with the notion. For too many human beings are pathetically set in their ways—except for new ideas in clothes and hair styles and the like.

In past years, many growers have come here to get a first-hand look at my mulched garden. One summer, more or less to see how many of these visitors would notice, I put some dirt on top of the mulch on my petunia bed. Quite a few of the callers asked why I didn't mulch that particular flower, and then I would push a bit of the dirt back and expose the hay.

If there have been arguments against planting potatoes and onion sets by merely tossing them on the ground and putting hay over them—instead of laboriously planting them the old way—I haven't heard any of the complaints. Also, as far as I know, no one has objections to the practice of putting hay on top of matured turnips and carrots and beets in your patch, then gathering them, when wanted, through the winter. It's best to use baled hay for this, since that's easier to manage.

A word of caution: after your soil has become so nearly perfect because of so much rotting mulch in it (I've used no other fertilizer for years), you may be swamped with the quantity of your crops. Just for instance: last summer I had to treat my KENTUCKY WONDER beans like limas—that is, let them mature, then shell them. No prob-

Scientists recreated a 9th-century onion and garlic eye remedy from an Anglo-Saxon manuscript and found that it killed 90% of antibiotic-resistant staph bacteria (MRSA).

lem, though; they were wonderful.

A few months ago, something happened which reminded me that I've gained a reputation of ignoring "authorities." One nice day a car drove in, two men got out, and when I went outside to speak to them, they were standing by my healthy holly bushes. One of the men said: "We're admiring these bushes, but, really, holly just won't grow in Connecticut!" I smiled and shrugged. Then the other man, with a grin, took it from there: "Experts do say that it won't, and that's no doubt why Miss Stout does it!"

WHAT 40 YEARS OF ORGANIC GARDENING HAVE TAUGHT ME

When I first started to have a garden, I naively accepted, for about 12 years, everything that experienced growers told me. For instance, it didn't occur to me to question the notion that the soil had to be turned over each year. And chemical fertilizer should, of course, be tossed around, even though you hated the smell. Then too, spray young plants with poison, however revolting that idea might be to you. I read garden books and magazine articles, trying not to notice that the writers often contradicted each other. Tomato and pea plants must be staked, at whatever cost of time and strength. And one also had to dig a long, deep trench — practically to China — for asparagus roots. (I could go on at length about the misinformation that was given me.)

And added to all the above, I naturally made any number of

There exists a kind of garlic called "solo garlic" which doesn't have separate cloves but is just one solid piece.

mistakes on my own. But even if I could remember every one of them, there would be nothing gained by listing them, although I believe I will mention a couple. One was that my plot, which was plowed each year, was at least 6 times larger than we needed, and after a couple of seasons I realized this. By that time, however, I had fed the very poor soil with manure and leaves and hated to abandon it, and I defy anyone to think up a more short-sighted attitude than that— unless, perhaps, it was another notion I had, to wit: Instead of growing a dozen tomato plants (which, since I wasn't canning or freezing anything, would have been ample for us), I put in a hundred of them, figuring that if a lot of them didn't produce, I would still have enough from those that did. In other words, instead of trying my best to grow a dozen plants properly, I spent time and energy on haphazardly fussing with a hundred.

The result of my faulty reasoning was that when that huge patch began to really produce the various items, I was confronted with incredible quantities of corn, strawberries, tomatoes, cucumbers, and on and on. And what I went through to try to dispose of them! Finally, I did find the courage and sense to abandon a lot of space, and my vegetable patch is now about 45 by 50 feet; this includes two rows of asparagus, some rhubarb, and six 30-foot rows of corn. The produce adequately provides for two for 6 months of the year, and frozen vegetables for us through the cold weather.

And here—as long as I've mentioned it—I think I will discuss what gardening has taught me about freezing my crops. If you feel that your own vegetables and fruits, which are eaten soon after being

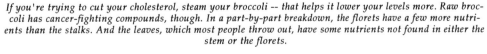

If you're trying to cut your cholesterol, steam your broccoli -- that helps it lower your levels more. Raw broccoli has cancer-fighting compounds, though. In a part-by-part breakdown, the florets have a few more nutrients than the stalks. And the leaves, which most people throw out, have some nutrients not found in either the stem or the florets.

picked, have more nutrition and flavor than those bought in a store, you may also agree with me that those which are frozen immediately after being gathered have the same advantages over the commercially-frozen ones. Asparagus was my husband's favorite vegetable, and yet he detected no difference in the taste of a freshly-picked serving as opposed to the frozen variety. It figures that an item you can put into the freezer about 10 minutes after it is brought in from the garden will hold flavor much better than if there is a somewhat longer delay, as there of course must be when the freezing is done in large quantity.

In my opinion, home freezing has 3 advantages over home canning, and one is that the flavor is better. Another is that the time required to do it is much shorter, and the third advantage is that it may very often happen that you can freeze something which you wouldn't dream of canning. For instance, you may pick a head of cauliflower which is twice too large for dinner, and although you could, of course, serve the rest tomorrow, perhaps you'd rather not, and you certainly wouldn't consider canning the surplus. But why not freeze it and serve it at some future time? As to asparagus, which must be gathered every day, maybe you're going out to dinner tonight, and, anyway, you may prefer not to serve the same vegetable so often. You wouldn't can a pound or two of asparagus, but you can pick it, steam it, and have it in the freezer all within 10 minutes. A quick rinse of the tender stalks under the water tap, and they are ready to be cooked.

Freezing directions say that beets don't take kindly to the process, but I find that they do if you cook them until tender, let them

We need potassium to help strengthen our muscles and control our blood pressure. Bananas are high in it, but they aren't the best source. Why not try a spud instead? Potatoes have more potassium. They don't have any fat and are a good source of vitamins and iron, too.

cool off, then put them into a container (probably cutting up some of them to save air space), and into the freezer. If you like Harvard beets, prepare them, freeze them, and just let them thaw when you want to serve them—if you prefer them cold, that is. Does cooking a beet so long before you freeze it deprive it of some food value? I don't know about that, but you ruminate over it while eating some super-market product which has no nutrient value whatsoever.

PLEASE—DON'T WORK SO HARD!

In a recent issue of a widely-read garden magazine (Ed. note—that's us she means, folks) there are at least 8 articles which make me feel like offering a helping hand to people who are working harder than they need to in order to grow things successfully.

First, there's this story about a man who does wonders with a compost pile, and there's a picture of his ton (yes, it said ton) of compost, ready to be distributed. The man is pictured, too, and he looks far from young, and I'm wondering how he'll make out when he gets really too old to be able to handle all that work. I can only hope that when that time comes, he will have found out it's quite unnecessary. All you need to do is put the leaves and hay and refuse wherever you want them, all over your garden and around your trees—for keeps.

And there's an article about how to defeat cabbage worms. The author says she first used trap crops without much luck, then tried spraying the plants with salt, which she felt that, for some reason, she had to do over and over. Also, she said this discouraged good insects,

Tomatoes are fruits. But, according to law, they're vegetables. Here's the juicy backstory: In the 1800s, New York's port taxed veggies, but not fruits. An importer wanting to cut costs went to court saying their toma-toes were fruits. The case went all the way to the Supreme Court, which ruled that, in "common language," produce often served with meats or fish is a vegetable. So, the man had to pay tomato tax.

but why, when there are so many other plants in a garden which aren't salted, should the insects mind not being able to do their stuff on the cabbage family plants? Then she tried dust, then rye flour, but didn't like these either, so she made an onion-garlic spray. But "the birds objected to that" (so she said, anyway), and she decided to put it on only every third or fourth day. She finally settled for sour milk, the effect of which "endures for the greater part of a week," but she admits that it doesn't get rid of every worm.

What's wrong with all the effort this woman went to, since it's good to experiment and discover how to defeat your plants' enemies? Well, what I can't understand is why just the salt treatment didn't do the job. Twice a season, or possibly three times, I go down my cabbage-family row and sprinkle a little salt from a shaker on each plant. I do it right after a rain or when there's dew on the plants, and it should be done, the first time, when the plants are young, then once or twice more if there's any indication of their being eaten. This has been my procedure for several years, during which time I haven't seen one cabbage worm.

There's a story about a man who grows peas, with the subtitle "Here's a system that can give you 3 successive pickings from a single planting of pea vines!" with an exclamation point after it—and I've always thought that 3 such pickings were routine. They are for me. Also, what this man goes through—rotary- tilling, fertilizing, wire fence, stakes—isn't necessary. Just plant your peas in a mulched soil, and the next step—pick 'em. The tall varieties can chmb up last year's corn stalks, and the dwarf ones can be kept off the ground with hay,

Trying to get more calcium? Instead of pouring another glass of milk, you could reach for the fruit bowl. Figs are high in calcium. A cup of dried ones has as much calcium as the same amount of milk. And unlike the cool drink, figs are also a great source of fiber.

which should be handy, anyway, for mulch. And some gardener says that he pulls up his potato plants, in order to pick little ones, then puts the plant back. If you will, in planting, lay seed potatoes on top of the soil and cover with leaves and hay, then you can merely lift the hay in order to pick tiny ones; the plant need not be disturbed.

And the idea of making a project out of growing earthworms puzzles me, since you needn't buy them or make a special effort to have them if you will keep your garden covered with mulch. You will automatically have all the earthworms you need. About the edible soybean story—why cultivate them? You don't need to. As for Spanish onions, you don't have to prepare the bed and add fertilizer and compost as one man says he does, contending that the secret of producing the largest onions is to plant in a 4-inch (in depth) trench, water if necessary, and that massive onions "need a deep, well-worked soil." Well, in that severe drought last year, my onions were simply planted in ground (not a trench) which was covered with hay, weren't watered, the soil wasn't "worked," and many of them grew to a pound and a half.

I think I'll go lie down now. I'm exhausted just from writing about all the unnecessary work that some people do.

MULCH CAN BEAT OLD JACK FROST . . .

Back in 1966, there may have been some who supposed my garden would be in trouble. My plot is in a frost pocket, and the month of May was abnormally cold for us that year. It was followed

About 40% of the corn grown in the USA is used for ethanol to add to fuel and another 40% is used for livestock feed.

by 7 nights of severe frost in June, the last one on the 22nd. Then came a killing frost on August 28th. Add to this, almost no rain all summer. And since I have a shallow well, I didn't dare water anything, which, altogether, sounds as though my garden couldn't have produced much, doesn't it? But it did.

My patch had clumps of baled hay along every row, and when frost threatened, it took a surprisingly short time to place the hay over the plants. However, just to have very cold weather until late June holds some things back, such as tomatoes and corn. My 35-year- old asparagus bed produced adequately, because I save it from freezing by always gathering it in the late after noon, then tossing hay on the tips that are just coming through.

We had more lettuce and parsley that season than we could use, although we ate both every day. There was a great abundance of lincoln peas in early summer and several meals of wando in September while string beans, both green and yellow, fairly dripped from the vines, and we cooked them when they were very young and tender. And my milkman, who is very fond of them, took quite a few home.

The root crops—carrots, beets and parsnips—did awfully well. Some of the single carrots were large enough to serve two or three people, and a few of the beets were the biggest I've ever grown. Kohlrabi, early cabbage and early broccoli were completely satisfactory, and Brussels sprouts did fairly well, but the rest of the cabbage family didn't have time to mature. Only one out of 6 plants of purple cauliflower made a head, and the white cauliflower failed completely. Late cabbage and kale were a flop.

Ounce for ounce, kiwis pack the biggest nutritional punch of any fruit in your produce aisle. They have twice the vitamin C of an orange, and they're another high-potassium, low-salt alternative to bananas.

Peppers, which I believe do best in hot weather, grew very well, but I had to gather them before they were ripe because of the August frost. And I had to do the same with the squash family, buttercup and BABY BLUE HUBBARD were the only varieties which matured before the vines were killed, but I gathered the whole crop and they're good, even though not fully developed. Our corn was ready by the first of August, and we had some until the second week of October. The tomatoes were very slow in ripening, but came through surprisingly, and I froze plenty—which is quite a few, since I go for frozen raw ones in a big way.

The bush limas, soy, and 4 kinds of climbing shell beans were more prolific than I've ever had before. And there were so many turnips in my patch that I'd have to hunt around for some people to give some to. Perpetual spinach, Chinese cabbage, beets, kohlrabi, Brussels sprouts—all were available in November and carrots, under bales of hay, for the winter.

My freezer had more vegetables in it than I could dispose of before spring.

I guess I don't need to remind you that since the weather was so uncooperative that season, none of the above would have been true if I hadn't had a mulched garden.

I still get frost when no one else around here does. But late this past spring there was one that hit others too. Not being used to it, they merely put bushel baskets and such over their tomatoes, peppers, etc., and didn't cover beets and cabbage—and they lost the lot. I'm used to big frosts in late May (even up to Mid- June) and I cover

Apples are a good source of fiber and vitamin C. As you take a bite of one, do you notice a sweet smell? Apples, pears, cherries, and plums are just some of the fruits that come from the same family tree as the rose.

everything (including peas and lettuce) with gobs of hay and it has always worked. I feel safe, but who knows? If Jack Frost figures out a way to sneak in under the hay, I think I'll forget gardening and resort to knitting.

. . . AND DEFEAT A DROUGHT

Many people have asked me if mulching adequately protects my flowers and vegetables from a severe drought. The answer is yes; through eleven seasons of year-round, over-all mulching, with several serious droughts, the only crop I have lost has been one late planting of corn. Now I believe I could have saved that too. And I have never watered anything in the vegetable garden except once: late corn just after I had planted it.

The following suggestions are for those of you who have not yet taken advantage of the tremendous benefits from a complete and constant mulch. Let us assume that the time is the middle of May and that somehow or other you know that there is a serious drought ahead. We have had so many in Connecticut of late years that this would be an almost safe assumption here.

With a little help the early crops will make it; spinach, lettuce, peas. The only thing you need to do for them is to gather together some leaves and hay and put six or eight inches of mulch around them. Shade the lettuce if you can. Three crops are saved.

You will get asparagus this year if you don't do anything, but, for the sake of next year's crop, it would be a pity not to mulch it too.

The rare European white truffle is the world's most expensive vegetable (if we considered mushroom as vegetables), with a price tag that can exceed 2,200 euros ($2,400) per 0.45 kilograms (1 pound).

Not leaves; they will mat and make it difficult for the asparagus to push through. Use hay; if you must, you can buy salt hay. It is rather expensive but it rots slowly and will last for a few years. If, however, you know a farmer who has "spoiled" hay (hay that has been wet and is unfit for food) the very best thing to do is to get a few loads of that. It rots more rapidly than salt hay, which is fine, for when it rots it enriches your soil. Of course if you have a scythe, a field of weeds or hay, and some ambition, you can cut your own mulch. Don't be afraid of weeds with seeds; in a heavy mulch they don't have a chance.

You can save your beets, carrots, parsnips and kohlrabi too. The very first thing is to thin them much more severely than you usually do. Then collect mulch (leaves, hay, weeds, garbage, sawdust, excelsior), and have it handy. Now give your plants a thorough wetting and at once put the mulch all around them six inches deep and between the rows. If the mulch is wet, too, so much the better.

This watering would not be necessary if you had had mulch on your garden all winter and spring. And you realize, of course, that the mulch not only conserves moisture but prevents weeds, which, during time of drought, are particularly harmful for they use up the moisture which the vegetables need so badly.

If you have already planted your bush beans, thin, water, and mulch them also. If you have not yet planted them, make a drill four inches deep; plant the beans sparsely; cover with two inches of dirt; water; cover with a board or cardboard, and mulch at once. You must take the board off just as soon as the beans sprout.

Hop shoots are eaten like asparagus (and even look like one), but the difference is that these shoots are very rare. They only emerge once a year during the spring and disappear quickly, which makes it hard to harvest in the wild. Hops are the herbs of beers, and the part that brewers don't use (the green tips of the hop plant) is called hop shoots. These are the 2nd most expensive vegetables in the world priced at 1,000 euros per kilogram, or about $1,100 per 2.2 pounds.

Since we are assuming that you have reason to expect a severe drought, don't plant pole beans. Instead, make successive plantings of bush beans and soak them overnight before you plant them.

If you have put in your first planting of corn, thin it to two plants in a hill instead of the customary three. Water it and give it six inches of mulch. If you run out of weeds, hay, leaves, sawdust, use as many layers of wet cardboard as you can muster. The cardboard is only an emergency measure; it is not, of course, as satisfactory as hay and leaves, because the latter rot and enrich your soil.

Even with a drought, I think you can still have late corn by planting it every ten days through June. Select the spot at once for these late plantings and mulch it six or eight inches deep with, in order of preference: hay, leaves, and weeds, sawdust, excelsior, old cartons and cardboard. All vegetable refuse is excellent; I haven't said much about it because kitchen garbage isn't very abundant and, since we are assuming you are an old-fashioned gardener who plows or spades instead of mulching, I am afraid you have disposed of last year's corn stalks, etc. If you have an unrotted compost pile, of course you will now spread that on the garden for mulch.

Each time you plant your corn, soak the seed overnight, make four inch drills and cover the seed with two inches of soil. Water thoroughly, put a board over the seed and mulch immediately.

Even if you have already bought your seed, I think you would be wise to abandon the mid-season varieties, such as Golden Cross Bantam, and put in the more quickly maturing kinds, such as North Star. The later varieties grow large and tall and require too much

Artichokes make other foods taste sweeter due to a chemical known as cynarin. This can be used to your advantage when pairing with wines that would otherwise be extremely dry.

moisture. Your very best bet is to plant Miniature and there isn't any sweeter corn, so why not? But don't plant it as closely as you normally would. Usually you can plant Miniature in rows two feet apart and plants one foot apart in the row; expecting a drought, I would give them a two by two spacing.

Now for the cabbage, broccoli, cauliflower, peppers, tomatoes. Your early cabbage will probably come through all right; simply mulch it heavily. Your late cabbage, cauliflower, and broccoli are probably not transplanted yet; put it very deep and four feet apart instead of three and mulch heavily. If the peppers and tomatoes aren't in, put them very deep too and farther apart than customary. But if they are already planted and you water and mulch them heavily (which means six or eight inches), you will probably get a good crop. I have never watered my tomatoes or peppers and yet, ever since I've used the over-all mulching system, I have always had good crops, even in a season when the lilac bushes began to droop. I prefer Blue Hubbard squash to any other, but if there was going to be a drought, I think I would settle for Butternut, which is excellent too. If you have used up all the better kinds of mulch, pile anything at all around the squash—anything which will keep the sun from baking the soil.

Whatever you use for mulch, the question arises: what if we get a nice shower but not a heavy rain? Won't the mulch prevent the water from reaching the plants? It does, of course. However, one little shower is not going to do hard-baked soil any good; lots of little showers will keep your mulch nice and damp; a heavy rain will go straight through the mulch. Whatever the clouds decide to do, you

The meaning of "vegetable" as a "plant grown for food" was not established until the 18th century. In 1767, the word was specifically used to mean a "plant cultivated for food, an edible herb or root." The year 1955 saw the first use of the shortened, slang term "veggie".

will be a great deal better off with mulch than without it.

About lawns. Well, you can't mulch them, of course. The only thing I know to do is not to cut them often or closely and don't rake them. The only adequate thing I know for a lawn in a drought is to water it and perhaps shade it. If you can't do that, you can at least remain optimistic and cheerful about it. Our lawn has sometimes been as brown as coffee from August to winter, but, as one writer who came to see my system said: "What's so ugly about brown?" Then in the spring there it is again, as green and hearty looking as ever.

What about your flowers? You will immediately mulch all of your perennials if you have not already learned to be kind to them by keeping them constantly mulched.

Do you grow sweet peas? They are supposed to require watering. I grow mine in the all-year-round mulched vegetable garden. I never water them and I have picked blossoms through summers when there was almost no rain at all for three months. But if you have a row of them and haven't kept them mulched and you are expecting a severe drought, my advice would be to abandon them for this year.

Asters, mulched, will come through sailing if they are planted in partial shade (which, the books tell us, they should be anyway). Most annuals will survive, if well mulched. Lobelia is an exception; it demands water (and mine gets it because I love it).

Petunias are the most satisfactory flower I know of in dry weather. Even before I had learned to mulch, when everything else gave up, the petunias held up their heads and bloomed.

All flower beds should be under a constant mulch, drought or

Tomatoes are the most popular vegetables in the world. It originated in the South American Andes around the area of modern day Peru and was first used as a food by the Aztec's in Southern Mexico.

no drought. You can easily do this without making them look ugly. Peonies can be mulched with dead leaves and their own tops. They grow so rapidly that very soon one doesn't see the debris around them.

If you don't want them to look untidy, roses need more thought. Well-rotted hay, mixed with crushed leaves, is good. Put it on six inches deep and then scat ter soil on top of it. It all looks like soil then, but the mulch is so deep that weeds cannot sprout. This is also satisfactory for large annuals, such as zinnias.

For small, low-growing annuals I use a fine mulch. Since I keep my whole vegetable garden mulched constantly there is always mate-rial there, not quite rotted enough to be rich soil but rotted enough to look like it. I put this around my small annuals. If you don't have such material you can use crushed leaves mixed with a little soil and wood ashes. This may sound like quite a job, but you have to do it just once a season. It is not as much work as spading up a flower bed and then hoeing it and weeding it all summer long. And it greatly en-riches your soil and keeps the moisture in the ground and carries you through a drought.

No doubt you have a favorite flower bed. Mine is a large circu-lar one full of phlox drummondi, with a border of lobelia. When the flowers are short of water, so is our well and for this pet of mine I keep a large watering pot by the kitchen sink. Into it goes all waste water except any that might have a little grease or too much soap in it. The water I rinse the dishes in, wash vegetables in, and so on; it is surprising how often I fill that watering pot even when I am being

Carrots were originally white or purple. The modern day orange carrot wasn't cultivated until Dutch growers in the late 16th century took mutant strains of the purple carrot and gradually developed them into the sweet, plump, orange variety we have today.

thrifty with the water.

Then there are your coffee grounds and tea leaves. These are wet and make good mulch. Mixed with earth, dead leaves, wood ashes, rotted hay they don't look unattractive. Guaranteed not to grow weeds.

So, if you have not been foresighted enough to mulch your garden in the autumn and are facing a serious drought, the very first thing to do is to get hold of all possible kinds of mulch and get the whole garden, both that part which is planted and that which is not, covered against the hot, drying rays of the sun. Manure is excellent, of course. If the town cuts the weeds and grass along the roadside, run out and rake it up. Kitchen garbage, all except meat scraps, is perfect. There is nothing offensive about vegetable garbage, you know, except our bad habit of keeping it in an airless container until it smells.

To sum up: mulching keeps the ground cooler than it would be otherwise, conserves the moisture, prevents the soil from baking, thus providing better aeration, and keeps the weeds from growing and robbing the vegetables and flowers from the nourishment and water which they need. As to spacing, there is just so much moisture to be had in a given area and therefore crowding is bad at any time but fatal in a drought.

The answer is to start now to establish an all-year-round overall mulching routine. It is highly advantageous at any time; it is a life saver in a drought.

First ancient civilization that truly incorporated garlic into their diet was Egypt. In 3rd millennium BC garlic was used not only by nobility, but also in medicine, religious rituals and was given to the slaves as a powerful source of strength.

CHAPTER 2.

My Answers to the "Experts

ON ADDING NITROGEN TO THE SOIL

One day (I don't know how many years ago this was) I read an article in an old and reputable farm paper saying that if you used fresh unrotted vegetable matter for mulch you must add nitrogen to the soil. I think the article was stronger than that; I think it tried to frighten you against doing anything so disastrous. I wasn't scared but I was interested.

I sent the article to a friend—an expert organic gardener—and asked how much of it I should believe. He told me to buy a bag of either cottonseed meal or soybean meal and sprinkle it about, particularly on lettuce and spinach. Also, I believe, on parsley, beets and corn.

I did this and my garden continued to thrive. I had heads of Great Lakes lettuce which were suitable only for families of nine or ten. When I wanted to make a salad for four people, say, I would sim-

Tomato plants over 6 feet tall, grown in nothing but rotted leaves for fertilizer and mulch.

ply pick a small part of a head, using the rest later.

Years went by and my garden flourished and I wrote articles and then a book about it and began to talk to garden clubs and other organizations. I found out that it is one thing to have a highly successful garden by using an unorthodox, no-work method, encouraging friends and neighbors to emulate you, and quite another to look an audience of 80 or so men and women in the eye and try to answer their questions intelligently. And answer letters from all over the country.

When a woman writes to me and asks: "Does it really work? I don't want to be laughed at," it is simple enough to write back: "Sure it works and what do you care if you're laughed at? People made fun of me for years; now I'm making fun of them. Your turn for laughing will come, don't worry."

But when someone asks some technical question, the answer to which I don't know, if it has to do with my kind of mulching I feel that I must do my best to find the right answer. Also, when I read something which flatly contradicts my own experience, I try to find out which one of us is on the wrong path.

An example of this second predicament was an article I read in the December 1955 issue of *Organic Gardening and Farming*. It was How I Get Free Mulch by Archer Martin and I found it an interesting and valuable article. But these two sentences bothered me: "The matter (meaning the mulch) should not be put down while still green during the growing season, for *it will rob the plants of nitrogen during its decomposition. This is a cautionary note that should be observed care-*

Marilyn Monroe was considered one of the most beautiful women in the world. One of her producers/photographers said she'd look beautiful "even in a potato sack," which gave them the idea for the shoot. The Idaho Potato Board agreed, and potato sales skyrocketed.

fully." The italics are mine.

I wrote to Mr. Martin, told him that I had put green (unrotted) matter on everything for thirteen years and had never had reason to think I shouldn't have, even during those years before I had used cotton seed meal to supply nitrogen. I asked him how he knew it was an unwise thing to do.

He wrote (saying that I might quote him): ". . . nitrogen is needed for the decomposition to take place, just as it is needed for the process of growing. Seemingly, the decomposition process is stronger than the growing process, for I've heard all my life that nitrogen for decomposition will be robbed from the plant trying to use it for growing."

Mr. Martin added that he was not a gardening expert and I felt that I had better look around for a more scientific opinion. Before I got around to it I read in the February 1956 issue of *Organic Gardening and Farming*, under Questions and Answers:

". . . you were right to apply cow manure — but the manure should have been well rotted. Fresh manures need nitrogen to aid the material to decompose, therefore the soil is deprived of the nitrogen content until the manures have decomposed and only then does the growing plant receive the nitrogen."

I haven't used manure for ten years because under my method my soil is so rich that I no longer need it, but when I used to use it I always preferred it fresh and found it satisfactory, so this note, too, was contrary to my experience.

I wrote, then, to two scientists, one of them con nected with a

Potatoes have almost all nutrients humans need to survive. To prove this, the Executive Director of the Washington State Potato Commission ate nothing but potatoes for 60 days.

large commercial seed house, the other, Professor Arthur J. Pratt, of the Department of Vegetable Crops, of Cornell University. Dr. Pratt sent me the Cornell Extension Bulletin No. 886. Since the letter from the seed house and the bulletin and Dr. Pratt's letter all said exactly the same thing in different words, I will quote only Dr. Pratt's letter, which he gave me permission to use.

He wrote: "Yes, leaves, hay, straw, etc., that are not decayed or that are only partially decayed will rob the soil of nitrogen if they are mixed into the soil. But when used on top the way you use them, I have never seen a nitrogen shortage as a result of the mulch. Of course, if there was not enough nitrogen in the soil in the first place the mulch materials do not add any for at least a long time, so they would not help a shortage nor add to it.

"I have never seen fresh manure, even when mixed with the soil, cause a nitrogen shortage. If it did it would be because of a large amount of straw mixed with it and the shortage would be very temporary. You could even get a temporary shortage from using cottonseed meal early in the season when the ground was cold and wet. The reason for it is, of course, that bacteria first have to break down the rather complicated organic compounds to make them available to the plant in the nitrate form. In doing that the bacteria use the readily available nitrogen for their own growth. In a few days to a few weeks they die and release that nitrogen to the crop." Since the answer of the scientists coincides with my own experience, I believe it. My quarrel with people who write about gardening (or any subject, for that matter) is that they often state as a fact something which they do not

Studies all over the world suggest that Brussel sprouts are world's most hated vegetable. American President George H.W. Bush famously hated Brussel sprouts so much he banned them from the White House. Recent studies have shown that your like or dislike of Brussel sprouts (and other cabbages) is encoded in your DNA.

know to be a fact. That is regrettable. Not counting all of the other advantages of my method, it has saved me thousands of hours of labor; think how unfortunate it is if those careless remarks about fresh mulch have prevented only one person— busy, old, not very strong, or merely lazy—from adopting this easy way of gardening!

I have had a number of letters from people who believe me, but are afraid my system won't work in their soil because it is heavy, while mine is light. I answer them by saying that a number of people here in Redding with heavy, sticky, clayey soil have tried my method and are delighted with the results. Also, I quote from the bulletin I mentioned above: ". . . this organic material loosens heavy soils and makes them easier to work and better aerated."

And now for you doubting Thomases who simply cannot believe that I have built up a fine, adequate soil by using nothing but rotting mulch for over ten years, and never digging it in, I want to quote from a letter which I received recently from R. F. Holt, assistant professor of agronomy of the University of Connecticut. Mr. Holt writes me:

"I have read your book and found it very interesting. I believe that a system such as yours has definite advantages particularly for the home gardener.

"I am enclosing a copy of your soil test report which indicates that your soil is well supplied with the major plant nutrients. The pH values are about perfect."

WHEN THE SCIENTISTS PAID ME A VISIT . . .

Unless your diet is seriously lacking in Vitamin A, carrots don't help you see better at night. The belief that eating them does improve night vision actually stems from a WWII propaganda campaign.

One day in spring four professors of agriculture from the University of Connecticut drove into our yard. One professor after another piled out of the car (every one of them young, pleasant, friendly, and even attractive).

We went to the vegetable garden; I like to think that they were impressed with my soil, black and rich from years of rotting mulch, but unfortunately not one of them was the gushing type. They pulled back the mulch and there were my allies, the earthworms, right on the job, and one professor said:

"Gosh, the other day I looked for half an hour and found only one earthworm to fish with."

Two of them began to whisper over the corn and I begged them not to be so secretive. So they told me that the striped leaves meant that there was not enough magnesia in the lime I was using. There were no weeds in the garden except some milkweed in the asparagus and I told them that I purposely left that because I liked it in salad. They said the roots went all the way to China and I might be sorry. The next morning out came the milkweed.

There wasn't one bean beetle to be seen and our visitors were surprised when I told them I had planted the seed about the 20th of May. They said if you waited until June to plant your beans you were less likely to have bugs. Speaking of bugs in general, one of them said that a healthy plant is safer from pests than an unhealthy one; he said he had seen this to be true over and over in fields of alfalfa.

We went to the flowerbeds, me hoping I might get a little

Unfortunately, the entire idea that spinach made you stronger was based on a simple notational mistake. In 1870, German chemist Erich von Wolf reported that a 100 g serving of spinach contained 35 mg of iron, far more than any other vegetable. And iron is associated with strength, as it helps carry oxygen to your muscles. The problem is that von Wolf had mistakenly misplaced a decimal point. 100 g of spinach contained the more modest and normal quantity of 3,5 mg of iron, not 35 mg.

praise for making them so attractive with my use of half-rotted mulch. No comment.

We went into the house and Fred gave the professors cocktails, which we hoped would loosen them up a bit. But scientists are cautious.

However, when I got up my courage and asked them what they thought of my method, three of them looked at the fourth, who probably was the big shot, and he said: "For flower and vegetable gardens, it seems to be an excellent idea."

That satisfied me.

In August Dr. Pratt came all the way to Connecticut to have a look. He is a man around fifty, I should think, and a home vegetable garden specialist who teaches courses in general horticulture. Fresh as I can get, on paper, about experts, I am just a little nervous when I meet them in the flesh. But here again I didn't need to be, for what an unusually nice, intelligent, and friendly person Dr. Pratt is! He took such a lively interest in, and was so sympathetic to, my method that it didn't occur to me to ask what he thought of it. Fred did ask him why people kept on plowing and he laughed and said: "Just because they always have, I suppose." Which is what I tell the garden clubs I talk to.

Later Dr. Pratt wrote me a letter in which he said:

. . your long experience with no plowing and fitting should be helpful to all of us. If good yields can be maintained for ten or fifteen years without plowing or fitting, they probably can be maintained forever on similar soils."

There is No Such Thing as a Negative-Calorie Vegetable
Even celery, usually touted as the best negative-calorie vegetable, and which is indeed mostly composed of water and fiber, still contains about 6 to 10 calories per stalk, yet digesting it requires only about ½ calorie.

I told Dr. Pratt that the Connecticut boys had said that my corn lacked magnesia. He said he didn't think so; he thought it lacked nitrogen. I had already given it some Dolomitic lime for magnesia shortage and was willing also to give it nitrogen, but I did ask this: "If it is lacking in either or both, why should I care since I get two fine ears from almost every stalk and since it has never been more delicious than it has this cold summer, weather which is supposed to be bad for corn?"

He grinned and answered: "You'd get bigger ears." Here is a peculiar thing: While a professor is talking to me I feel humble, trusting him utterly, but let him get out of my sight and I begin to think: "Well, interesting, if true." Now that the University of Connecticut and Cornell scientists are all back home where they belong, I don't feel quite sure that I know what my corn lacks. If anything.

Dr. Pratt took samples of soil away with him and I received a letter from him saying that it was short of nitrogen and too alkaline. I had been negligent about giving it cottonseed meal last summer and had dumped a lot of wood ashes on it to get rid of them. After all, when you are so busy telling everybody else how to garden, where can you find time to practice what you preach? Even so, I had had excellent crops, considering the late June frost, the early September one, and the awfully cold summer. The upshot is that I have been asked to cooperate next season and run some tests. I will put cottonseed on two-thirds of the vegetable garden; one-half of the remaining third will get ammonium nitrate and the other half will get nothing at all. About this Dr. Pratt wrote me that this might tell us "what form and

For quite some time, people avoided eating anything from the nightshade family because they considered them to be deadly poisonous. In addition to tomatoes, the family includes potatoes, eggplants, and peppers. However, this belief was challenged when people were eating a lot of these vegetables out of desperation during a time of famine and nothing happened.

how much nitrogen should be added with a grass-hay mulch." Now all you organic gardeners had better get busy and pray for our side!

Scientists are going to be coming more than once and from more than one institution, I behave, during the growing season, to see how everything is making out. And I honestly don't believe that the chicken and dumplings I gave Dr. Pratt last August has a thing to do with his intention to come, even though he did say that my chicken and dumplings are pretty darn delicious.

Among the letters I get from people everywhere, there are quite a few from women who are a little desperate, who write: "My husband and all my friends are making fun of me and laughing at me because I'm gardening your easy way."

I am particularly grateful to Dr. Pratt and the other professors for now I can write to these women and tell them:

"The scientists aren't laughing!"

WHEN THEY CRITICIZE ORGANIC GARDENING . . .

Well, my organically-minded friends, you may as well face it: you are faddists, practicing witchcraft. This must be true, because the scientists say so, and whoever heard of a scientist making a misstatement?

I have before me a 17-page, 9-by-12-inch booklet, printed on slick paper, which is called "Science Versus Witchcraft." On the cover, which has a blue-green background, the word "Science" is in large but dignified white letters (pure), the "Versus" is black, small

At one point in history, the Egyptians created something like a tampon that was made from dried vegetable fibers, papyrus, and cotton.

and inconspicuous, the "Witchcraft" is big, black, menacing and sort of erratic—quite "witchy" looking. At the bottom, in much smaller print, is the following: "Reprinted from Plant Food Review, a publication of the National Plant Food Institute, 1700 K Street, N.W., Washington, D.C.

The booklet is rather expensively gotten up—there are pictures, and some green color used throughout which, I am told, costs more to print than plain black and white.

On the inside cover there is a list of contributors. Twenty-eight of them are employed at various universities or colleges; three are connected with the Department of Agriculture, and one is an agricultural consultant. On the first page of the booklet is an unsigned foreword, which is short (581 words), yet the writer labels organic gardeners "faddists" 7 times; he also calls them "self-styled experts," says they suffer from the "organic farming bug," that they "prate," and states that they have the faddist approach to good nutrition, rather than the "sane and sensible" one. (You may have one guess as to who has the latter.)

We will come back to this foreword, but let's now turn to the next article of 5 pages, also unsigned, but quoting from the various experts listed. There is this, for instance; "The question of 'chemical versus organic' origin of plant food is one of the easiest to deal with in hard, cold, scientific facts as . . . (here there are a few names of 'authorities') ... so effectively prove .. The word "prove" is also used in the second paragraph of the foreword.

In almost any scientific book, the author, more likely than not,

---

Supposedly if you make a mistake writing with a pen, you can use the outside skin of a cucumber to erase it.

states (at some point or other) something like this: "Back in 1900 they (the scientists) thought this-and-that—ha! ha!—but now we know . . It doesn't seem to occur to the writer that in say, the year 2000 (or maybe in 1975) some "expert" may write about this scientist's "fact": "Up to 1975 it was thought that so-and-so was true—ha! ha!—but we now know . . In other words, a scientist seems always to know, and anyone who disagrees with him is a faddist, not to mention a witch.

We now come to: "Organic matter is neither essential nor necessary for plant growth." Let's skip for a moment to page 13 of the booklet where another scientist says: "Organic matter is desirable and essential for maintaining favorable physical conditions in cultivated soil." Don't these two statements contradict each other? It does seem that these two gentlemen should have gone into a huddle and compared notes, since the whole point of this rather expensive propaganda was to boost chemicals, not organic matter.

The next point this article makes is so negative that it really is a bit on the pathetic side. The writer speaks of experiments which were "conducted to compare the effects of 'organic' and 'inorganic' sources of plant foods on nutritional factors of fruits," and he mentions two; one showed "only minor differences in vitamin C content," the second "no significant differences in vitamin C content and other nutritional factors measured." And then: "Other studies have shown that the content of such common nutritional elements as calcium, phosphorus, iron and copper in fruits is influenced only slightly by fertilizer treatment."

I don't know what anyone else might conclude from this, but

Carrots and other orange vegetables are high in beta-carotene which is what gives them the color. If you ingest too much beta-carotene it will actually enter your bloodstream and since it does not get broken down in the body it gets deposited on the skin. The medical term for this is called carotenemia which sounds more intense than it is since the condition is harmless and eventually your skin will break down the color and return to normal.

my guess is that certainly whatever good "influence" there was here must have been on the organic side; otherwise the wording would have been different, and one can't help wondering just how minor, insignificant and slight these differences were. It does seem that the writer would have done better to have skipped that factor.

Next there is a reference to Holland: ". . . the most concentrated use of commercial fertilizer in the world is in Holland. And on the average Hollanders live longer than any other people . . . This certainly indicates that food grown with chemical fertilizer cannot be very unhealthful." I, for one, am allergic to jumping to conclusions, and what a leap that is! However bad (or good) an opinion one may have of chemical fertilizer, no one can possibly think it is the only thing that affects one's health. How much exercise do Hollanders get? How much do they drink? How tense are they? How much adulterated food do they eat, and how much of it is poison-sprayed? Do they overeat? I am sure you can think up other questions to add to mine. No, the writer certainly shouldn't have used that argument.

The next to last paragraph in the booklet reads: "Fertilization of more and more of our present crop and pasture acreage and even some of our forest land will continue, because it's the only practical way of satisfying the nutrition requirements of these crops where a soil deficiency occurs. For this reason the fertilizer industry will have a larger and more important role than it has ever had in supplying the increased demand for its products."

With this in mind, let's go back to the foreword, where we find this:both faddists and opportunists have grabbed the chance to step

Potato plants were taken into space into 1996 on the Columbia space shuttle where they were the first vegetables grown in space. According to NASA, these "Quantum Tubers" involved "combining an agricultural technique from China with controlled environment technologies originally developed by the University of Wisconsin-Madison for plant growth in space."

up their attack on the use of 'chemicals' of any kind in food-production or processing." (Here he seems to include the sellers of organically-grown food, as well as the growers of it.) Notice the indicated difference between the man who makes a living selling fertilizers and one who sells, let us say, "natural foods." The former is concerned in an industry, the latter is an opportunist. The one is playing an important role, the other is grabbing a chance. Oh me!

One of the "authorities" has this to say: "The maintenance of permanent soil productivity requires that fertilizers and lime be used to correct the deficiencies resulting from continued cropping, leaching, and erosion losses." Although I didn't set out to argue any one point in the booklet, I do want to say a word or two about the preceding 4 lines, but I am merely stating a fact, about which there is no room for argument. For the past 19 years I have used no fertilizer (and incidentally, no poison sprays) except some cottonseed meal; for the past 7 years I have used no lime, and for the last 3 years not even cottonseed meal, with the exception last winter (because of being a coward and very crazy about corn) of some meal on half of my corn plot; I can't remember which half, however. I keep hay and leaves on my garden all year round; these rot and nourish the soil. When I sent a sample of my dirt to the Connecticut Agricultural College (Storrs) to be analyzed; the pH value was satisfactory, and all the other necessary elements came out High, Very High, or Very, Very High.

If anyone has gotten the idea that this attractive- looking pamphlet has disturbed me, he is mistaken. Quite the contrary. For instance, when I saw a feature article in the Rural New Yorker some

Out of all the vegetables, asparagus loses it's flavor the fastest, especially after it has been cut. It's best to eat it the day you buy or it, or else store it in the refrigerator with a damp towel wrapped about the bottoms of the stalks to keep it moist for a couple days.

time ago entitled "Plowing IS Important," I was pleased because I figured that quite a few people must have abandoned plowing or it never would have occurred to anyone to write such an article. So when I saw a lot of "experts" taking the trouble to try to convince growers that they must use chemical fertilizers, and are stooping to name- calling, I think; So enough people are going in for organics to get the "experts" nervous! That's fine! Three cheers for the faddists and opportunists, and hats off to the witches!

ON USING PLASTIC MULCH . . .

In writing about gardening, I try very hard to stick to my own experiences, but when it comes to using plastic mulch I admit freely that I have no personal experience. However, all one needs, in my opinion, in order to be able to figure out what's wrong with plastic mulching, is a little imagination and a little common sense.

Let's say that a person, who was rather short changed when imagination was being passed around, decides to use a plastic mulch instead of hay on a garden the size of mine (45x50); he figures that, for one thing, the plastic will cost less, since it lasts forever. Well, here's news for him. Plastic won't be cheaper because, since it doesn't supply the nourishment needed to keep a garden producing, he will also have to buy fertilizer each year to make sure that his plants get what a mulch of hay gives them; the hay rots and provides the soil with all the required nutrients.

I haven't used any fertilizers at all for 20-odd years, and have

If you shy away from onions because they make your breath smell, you might want to reconsider that life choice. Onions contain over 100 different sulfide containing compounds that can do everything from help control asthma to prevent certain types of cancer. The phytochemicals in onions might be able to prevent gastric ulcers. The chromium in them helps to regulate the blood sugar, and the sulfur also helps lower the blood sugar by increasing the production of insulin.

had much better crops than when I was gardening the old-fashioned way. One man, after he read my first book and then tried the mulch method, wrote me that it was obvious, when you figured it out, that rotting hay was better even than manure for growing things, for the latter contained only what was left of the former after the cows had been nourished by it. Well, my plants were doing so well that I didn't need that proof myself, but it was a good point to make to people who were hesitating about trying something new.

And of course all other vegetable and organic matter that rots—straw, leaves, corncobs, wood chips, kitchen garbage—will nourish your soil; cornstalks and the tomato, bean, asparagus plants should all be left on your plot, in order to do their share of providing nutrients.

As you no doubt know, the "experts" say that peat moss can't be counted on to furnish nourishment in soil, and for once I behave them, but please don't ask me why I do.

I have heard it said that there is less to do in a garden if you use a plastic mulch rather than an organic one, and I wonder how growers operate when using the former. Since it seems to be less work, I suppose they just spread the plastic on their plot in strips, then ignore the whole thing.

For the moment I am going to pretend that for some odd reason I've decided to use plastic for mulch on my 45-by-50-foot plot. Let's say that I put down strips of plastic, leaving a small space between, and I drop the seeds in the exposed area. But first I must do something about enriching the soil, and maybe buy some organic fer-

When our bodies bleed they have to be able to clot properly to stop the bleeding, and sometimes this can be a bit of an issue. Believe it or not, the cayenne pepper is actually capable of helping this happen. You can literally sprinkle it directly onto a wound where it will function as some sort of a spicy gauze and will stop the bleeding.

tilizer. But what? Manure? And do I make a compost pile? I'll certainly skip that, for it's quite a lot of work to get the materials together. Then, when the pile has become rich soil, I'd have to load a wheelbarrow with it and distribute it all around. Well, that whole routine is "out of bounds," as far as I'm concerned.

Now I go ahead and put in the seeds in my plastic- mulched garden and the plants show up and so do the weeds—in the spaces between the plants right in the rows which have to be made rather far apart. That is, the corn does, and potatoes, and squash, and tomatoes and, in fact, almost all the plantings. The question of weeds isn't a problem, of course, if you use an organic mulch. The hay, or whatever you use, is lying there in the row, as well as alongside it, and will keep just about all weeds from getting anywhere.

At last, the first summer of plastic-mulching my plot is over, and finally another spring shows up—time to plant early crops. But when I go out to the garden. I'm nonplussed; I can't get rid of the idea that the plastic, which was supposed to save me a lot of work, should certainly be moved to other areas. Why do I feel that? Well, I keep thinking of that good earth under the plastic, and it seems absurd not to make any use of it. And the small open space, which I used for planting last season, doesn't seem to be adequate now, so the only thing to do is to move those black strips to other spots, and that would certainly be a tedious job. (I will admit that maybe I am being unreasonable, and that it may be quite all right to cover up a lot of your soil with plastic and never produce anything in those areas, but the whole idea sounds goofy to me.)

That warm feeling from hot peppers is measured in units that honour the man who discovered the complicated way to measure the heat of peppers. Pepper heat is measured in Scoville Units in honour of Wilbur Scoville who invented the scale in 1912.

However, if a person is wise enough to use organic matter for mulch, all he has to do in early spring if he wants to plant some lettuce and parsley in whatever spot he may choose, is just pull the hay aside (if he hasn't already done that in the fall) and put in the seeds.

About asparagus, I just can't believe that anyone at all familiar with how this vegetable operates would use plastic in that bed. Asparagus likes to wander around and come up wherever it pleases. And it likes a rich soil—just as weeds do, unfortunately. But an organic mulch will, as I said, dispose almost entirely of the latter. As you may know, asparagus stalks can, and will, push up through a hay mulch, which they could of course never be able to do if your plot is mulched with plastic.

You also may know that air, rain, dew and sun reach the soil right through organic mulch. A plastic covering keeps all of these beneficial things from reaching the earth, although it's true that plastic will keep the ground damper than it would be if the soil stayed bare. But hay and leaves not only keep the earth moist, but also let dew and rain enter the soil, and help to hold the moisture in.

Since I started to use organic mulch, we have had several seasons with long droughts—one summer no rain at all for three consecutive months. Although I can't water any plants in dry weather because my well is very shallow, yet I didn't lose one vegetable through those dry spells. Squash needs lots of water, but despite that season with a three-months' drought, I had an oversupply.

Yesterday, when one of my neighbors (a confirmed organic gardener and mulcher) dropped in, I spoke of this article about plas-

Black walnut trees exude a toxic material from their roots to exclude other broad-leaved plants (including their own seedlings) from growing nearby and providing competition. They exude a toxic substance called Juglone.

tic. Although I knew she didn't use it, I asked her if she could think of anything at all in favor of it as a mulch, (As I said, I dislike holding forth about anything outside my own experience, and it never does any harm to try to be fair.)

My neighbor said that plastic is supposed to warm up the soil more quickly than hay. When I asked why she thought this, she hesitated for a moment, then said that someone must have told her it did. "Well, even if it does, what's so important about that?" I asked. "You can, for instance, plant lettuce on frozen ground, and it doesn't seem to mind. After all, it's only early plantings that need warmed-up soil; the sun does the job for later crops. So for parsley, lettuce, peas, all you need to do is take the hay off those areas in the fall and, in my experience, the ground is then never too cold to interfere with desired results."

She had one more suggestion which she thought might be favorable, and that was that since squash plants take up so much room in a garden, black plastic might make it easier to keep down weeds between the hills. However, I plant squash between my two rows of asparagus, and I've already said why I wouldn't use plastic for the latter, even if I went a little haywire and wanted to do so.

There is one other thing which would keep me from using plastic for mulch, and that is that a hay covering outwits (and don't ask me why) practically every weed except lamb's-quarters and milkweed and purslane. Which in my opinion is a sort of miracle, for those particular weeds are good eating, either in salad or cooked. In fact, lamb's-quarters is said to have more nutrient value than almost

The oil from the roots of a tree native from Maine to New York and Michigan and south to East Texas and central Florida was originally used to flavour root beer. This tree with mitten shaped leaves is called Sassafras.

any vegetable.

ON PLOWING, FREEZING AND OTHER IDIOTIC IDEAS . . .

Merchants who sell fertilizers and plows and so on aren't in sympathy with my ideas of gardening. One farm magazine published a lead article headed "Plowing IS Important." The writer went on at great length, citing technical data with the emphasis on the need to aerate the soil. He didn't seem to know (or just didn't want to admit) that in a plot which is well-supplied with humus, the earthworms do an efficient aerating job. I wrote an answer to that article, which the same magazine printed, asking "Why doesn't the ground under asparagus, rhubarb, perennial flowers, need to be aerated? And should one plow up one's rose bushes and trees each year, in order to aerate the soil under them?"

There is one thing I have learned — that people can say rather foolish things when they are determined to prove a point. One highly-respected garden writer said, in one of his books, that year-round mulching is bad because mulched plants freeze when others don't, and his "proof" was that a man he knew lost his mulched tomato plants one night from frost, while the un mulched ones of another gardener, only a mile or so away, withstood the cold. Well, this is, of course, nonsense; my garden happens to be in a frost pocket and my tomato plants will freeze when those across the road from me don't — yet both are mulched.

And I wish I had even a quarter for every "authority" who has

Zinnia flowers come in a rainbow of colours. What unusual colour is the one called 'Envy'? 'Envy' is a delicate shade of green.

said that it is virtually impossible to grow a gardenia successfully in your home—but how would I dispose of all that money? My gardenia plant is taller than I am, has had over 200 blossoms on it this last spring and summer, and it spends most of its life in my living room. And many cuttings from this plant, which I have grown for friends, are doing very nicely, thank you, in their homes.

An authority on almost any subject apparently finds it difficult to say, "I don't know." When I talk to a garden club, I sometimes warn the audience: Read one garden book, if you must, but better not make it two, for they are almost sure to contradict each other, then you're sunk. I am so conscious of all the unreliable advice and "information" that's bandied about, that when I write or talk to a group about gardening, I try never to advise, but simply to report that I did this or that, then state the outcome.

Using the mulch method, one learns that neither a chemical nor organic fertilizer is needed. Only rotting vegetable matter is required. I tossed cotton-seed meal around on my plot for a few years, but have discontinued that, and I have used no lime for the past 12 years. For years I haven't rotated my crops, and as far as I can tell, they couldn't care less.

I grow potatoes by merely laying the seed variety on top of the ground and covering them with hay. (Since I have heard that potatoes sold for eating are often sprayed to keep them from sprouting, I make sure to always get the seed kind for planting.) I plant onion sets by scattering a quart of them around, then placing hay on top of them, all of which requires not more than 10 minutes of time. You can save

A voracious green caterpillar can reach 4 inches (10 cm) in length while devouring many items in the vegetable garden. This is the tomato hornworm, which is a sight to see and hear chewing.

space by planting peas between the corn hills, by making double rows of lettuce, parsley, beets, carrots, and so on, and skip the job of transplanting by just dropping a few seeds of the cabbage family a foot or so apart, then thinning to one plant. And set out tomato plants against the wire fence. Then, instead of going to the bother of tying them to it, lay chunks of baled hay against the plants; this will hold them up.

And what about insects in a mulched garden? Well, for a number of years I have put cigarette ashes in the hill where I plant squash and have never had a borer. Also, I sprinkle salt on all young plants of the cabbage family and the result: no worms. I had done nothing at all for any other insects without ever losing a crop, until a spring a few years ago which is a sad tale and I will make it as short as possible. Through the years I have outwitted cutworms simply by keeping the mulch pushed up close to the plants, but when 3 plantings of lettuce didn't come up that spring, and my parsley, beets, carrots and spinach disappeared when they were about one-quarter of an inch high, I telephoned our agricultural agent and asked what he thought could be the trouble. He came here and investigated and found that my plot was infested with cutworms.

The agent told me that cutworms have learned some new tricks—attacking plants before they even show above the ground— and the answer was to dust or spray rotenone. And since I found no other solution in my *Organic Gardening Encyclopedia*, I had a choice between using rotenone (which is a plant-derived compound) or losing my whole crop and having to eat commercially-grown and no doubt

Baking soda gives you sweeter tomatoes
When sprinkled to your soil, baking soda decreases the acidity levels of the soil. In turn, sweetens up your tomatoes.

poison- sprayed vegetables. So I decided in favor of the former. In the weeks that followed, I discovered that cutworms were pestering many gardeners.

I have learned a number of things through the years which I haven't the space to list here. They've taught me that no matter how sure you feel that you have some problem solved, you probably couldn't be "wronger."

WHEN VISITORS COME CALLING

When I received a letter from the editors one spring saying an issue of *Organic Gardening and Farming* would carry an article called: "Fifty Places to Visit" and that my garden would be included, I began to strut a little.

Fred, my husband, who probably felt that living with a conceited woman would be just about the last straw, said: "Very likely there are only 50 organic gardens in the U. S. which *Organic Gardening* knows about specifically." His next contribution was: "You are going to be asked 5,000 questions that you can't answer." I said "So? Well, I've got what it takes to say, 'I don't know' 5000 times." He was right about the questions. I have only one thing to offer gardeners: my personal experience in growing flowers and vegetables with an over-all, year-round mulch. No plowing, harrowing, spading, weeding, hoeing, cultivating; no compost pile, no commercial fertilizer—labor reduced to an unbelievable minimum. I hope I will not sound immodest if I add that this seems to me to be enough for one person, and I am not in the least embarrassed when someone asks me, for in-

There are 10,000 different varieties of tomatoes. Sixty million tons of tomatoes are produced every year. Tomatoes are grown by about 86% of households growing their own food.

stance, what is the best way to grow African violets and I am obliged to answer: "I don't know." It is beside the point that I don't think anyone knows. However, if people were going to come and look around, I thought I had better get on my toes.

The mulched flower beds didn't look quite as neat and tidy as I had claimed they could be, so I dolled them up a little. Here and there a weed poked its nose through the mulch in the vegetable garden; I made short work of them by tossing some hay on them.

Before the issue of *Organic Gardening and Farming* came out, I received a letter from Mrs. Wilson Morse of Blandford, Mass., who had read my article about mulching in Prevention magazine and she asked to visit my garden. She and her husband arrived in a timid rain one morning in June. It was chilly, so we had a pot of coffee before going out into the drizzle.

I was thrilled at their lively interest, and when we returned to the house, Mrs. Morse produced pencil and paper from her bag, asked questions and wrote down my answers. She and her husband both gave me the feeling that they intended to hurry home and cover their garden with mulch.

Early in July visitors began showing up almost every day. I do wish I could mention them all, for every visit was interesting in one way or another. For instance, there were the two young men who brought me a sunflower in a pot, not knowing how appropriate it was; I was born in the Sunflower State.

There were the Shepards from Newtown, accompanied by the McEwens from Valley Stream, N.Y, Mr. McEwen knew his stuff and I

The first know greenhouse in history can be dated back to Rome during A.D. 30. The greenhouse was to provide Emperor Tiberius with his daily fresh cucumbers.

had a hard job keeping up with him, but I liked him immensely and when we parted, he seemed converted—a full-fledged mulcher, Mr. Shepard teased me. When I remarked that I was 71 and gardening this easy way I expected to keep at it until I was 90, he asked: "And what are you going to play around with after you're ninety?"

Helen Hadley came. She was also listed in the "Fifty Places to Visit." I had heard of her wonderful garden and was a little nervous when she called and asked to come, but she was lovely. She is the kind of person who really does something about anything she believes in. For instance, when she read my book she approved so highly of my method that she bought 25 copies—to "spread the good tidings." Later, we met Frank, her husband and saw their attractive, interesting place. The animals they are going to eat later on are fed organically-grown food.

The Greenawalts from Kutztown, Pa., were a great treat. Like so many of the others, the Greenawalts aU but embraced me when I assured them that with over all, year-round mulching, a compost pile is unnecessary. They could see for themselves that this was true; all they had to do was push back the mulch and see the wonderful richness of the soil. They could hardly believe it when I said I hadn't used any manure for eight or nine years—nothing but leaves and hay spread over the surface, never dug in.

Earl Dumas came—a man with years of experience in truck gardening, although now his specialty is trees. On the way out to the garden he said: "I approve of organic gardening, but it's too much work."

World Naked Gardening Day (WNGD) is an annual international event generally celebrated on the first Saturday of May by gardeners and non-gardeners alike.

He pulled back some mulch, picked up a handful of the soil underneath, gazed at the flourishing corn, tomatoes, parsley, then said: "I gave up my vegetable garden because I just couldn't find time for it." Then he glanced at me and thoughtfully added: "You haven't plowed for 12 years? And you use no chemical fertilizer, no manure, no compost pile. It's amazing—just has to be seen to be believed. This will revolutionize truck gardening. I'm sure going to grow vegetables again next spring."

Of course such a reaction from an experienced, seasoned gardener was about the biggest thrill I could have.

But there was another type of gardener which gave me another kind of thrill—the garden club woman. When the program chairman of the Westport Club telephoned and asked me to speak at one of their meetings, I felt diffident. When she added that their president would like to come and see my garden, I was more than diffident, feeling sure that garden clubs were too la-de-da to take to my practical but far-from-fancy method.

A few days later, Mrs. Murray Morse, the president, drove in with a car full of members. She couldn't have been nicer, and when she eventually introduced me at their meeting, she actually spoke as if she had been impressed with the appearance of my garden.

They all asked a lot of questions about vegetables and afterwards I said to one of the members: "I had the impression that garden clubs were chiefly interested in flowers," and she replied: "We don't grow vegetables simply because we haven't the time, and labor has become so expensive and hard to find. I'm sure many of us will have

To keep potatoes fresh and prevent sprouting, put an apple in the bag with the potatoes.

a vegetable garden now, since you've shown us how to do it with so little work." I have had this same experience over and over with garden clubs.

As the summer grew hotter and drier, I became more and more uneasy when a car drove in, although I love taking people to the garden and pushing back the mulch to expose the soft moist earth and the happy earthworms, grateful to me for giving them such fine soil to work with. But by the first of August, when all the rain we had had here in the valley was one June drizzle and one inadequate thunderstorm, I expected, each time I exposed the earth, to find it dry. But it stayed moist, and in one way that severe drought was to my advantage in my effort to prove my point for, oftener and more often, my visitors would say:

"Our garden has all dried up this year. We certainly will try your system."

Bess and Wilson Morse drove down again from Blandford and brought Irene and Leonard Mason with them. Irene has a column in the Springfield Union and had written with enthusiasm about my method, but Leonard is one of those people who are willing to wear themselves out because they like to see the dirt between their vegetable rows.

However, Irene had cornered him and read parts of my book aloud to him, and in spite of himself he got interested in my permanent strawberry bed.

We have been to Blandford twice since, and the Morses have a beautifully-mulched garden. But Leon ard is still holding out, with

There are more than 7,000 varieties of apples worldwide. About 2500 varieties exist in the U.S.

nothing mulched but asparagus and strawberries; we tell him that when old age catches up with him, he'll join the ranks. Whenever the radio stations around here have asked me to talk, it meant a continuous stream of prospective mulchers for several days, and after such a talk one Sunday morning, a car with a Florida license turned in at our place. One of the Connecticut visitors who had just arrived said: "Perhaps you had better talk to that Florida crowd first. They probably rushed up here after an early breakfast and would like to get back home before dark."

I suppose it was only natural to feel flattered when people from Ohio, Florida, Pennsylvania, Massachusetts drove in. Of course they were on their way to some vacation spot, or were touring New England, but just the same it gave me some satisfaction.

Of course, I would hke to be able to state that my method of gardening is infallible, that in spite of unprecedented heat and the severest drought we have ever had, my visitors saw a perfect crop. But I'm afraid I couldn't get away with that; many of my callers may read this book.

So here is the truth: I have never had finer corn than I did that summer; I tried a new variety—Joseph Harris's Wonderful and it lived up to its name. My tomatoes were fine, beets were never better, and parsnips, Chinese cabbage, beans, peas, spinach, soy beans, kale were as good as I've ever grown, and my lettuce, parsley and onions were wonderful.

But the pepper plants, which looked very healthy, didn't begin to produce until quite late in the season; finally I had plenty but they

John Chapman (aka Johnny Appleseed) was a nurseryman who planted apple orchards in Illinois, Indiana, Kentucky, New York, Pennsylvania and Ohio.

didn't mature early enough to ripen.

Most of the cabbage family was very temperamental, too, and the carrots took a sabbatical. And when I had just published a book saying I hadn't seen a Mexican bean beetle for years, which was true, they chose this summer to hold a large convention on both my string and lima beans.

But the rich moist earth I was able to exhibit after months of drought, the splendid crops of many things, persuaded practically everyone, I think, that I was on the right track. At the same time, the fact that I wasn't trying to pretend that anyone, ever, could always have a perfect garden, probably convinced most of the people that the claims I did make were valid. I think my mishaps helped my cause.

And, too, who wants to have a lot of headaches with his garden, then go see someone else's which hasn't had a single setback? Of course people arrive with doubts in their minds about no plowing or spading, but when they see a garden which hasn't been either plowed or spaded for 25 years producing many fine crops in soft rich earth, and against the worst odds, they believe.

Do try to believe that you needn't ever turn over your garden soil. Let the earthworms earn their board and keep.

GIVING REX SOME SISTERLY ADVICE

When my brother Rex and I were on a radio program together long ago we got into a tangle, which stopped just short of a hair-pulling match, because he contended that gardening was hard work

There are over 40,000 varieties of beans. Beans can be made into burgers, cakes, drinks, pies, fudge, muffins, jewelry, bean-bag chairs, toys, and musical instruments.

and there was no way to get around this. However, we do agree in general, and when I asked him to come over to lunch and talk about flowers, I thought I would probably go along with most of his comments.

To put him in the best possible humor I fed him the Stout National Dish: navy beans simmered for hours with a hunk of salt pork. Then we got into comfortable chairs, and he began;

"Of all the activities a man can spend his time on, gardening is about the only one which is certain to present him with a bewildering succession of delight and dismay." So far, so good, but he added: "If, after my 30 years of trying to nurse hundreds of plants into vigor and bloom I was asked to give useful advice to an aspiring gardener, I would tell him to always expect the dismay; then the delight, when it comes, will be a glorious surprise."

My system (or temperament) is just the opposite; for goodness' sake, expect delight. If dismay is what you get, it will be a jolt, yes, but think of all the wonderful expectant hours you spent! And the dismay needn't last long; in no time at all you find yourself anticipating fresh delights.

Rex went on to say that certainly you must never expect a particular delight to repeat itself, and I had to agree with this. He illustrated: "A few years ago I acquired three plants of a new variety of penstemon, and put them in a likely corner of a border. When they bloomed the following year they were really spectacular, and some week-end guests were so indelibly impressed that the following year, on the proper date, they unexpectedly arrived with a whole gang of

European settlers brought with them a recipe for "Bilberry Muffins". Bilberries were not to be found in the New World. Wild blueberries, native to the Americas, were both plentiful and delicious. The wild blueberries were substituted for Bilberries, and the Blueberry Muffin recipe was created.

their friends, to show them what a genius Stout was with penstemon; what they saw was one or two scraggly, spinding miseries, with neither bud nor bloom nor prospect of any."

He went on to say that he was just about convinced that plants have their own laws, and that they dislike, even bitterly resent, man's attempt to devise and estab- hsh sets of rules which vegetation is supposed to follow. Even if the man-made laws are empirical, if they're based on long observation of the conditions under which this or that vegetation is supposed to thrive, plants still don't like the idea; they don't want man presuming to tell them where and how to get along.

"To demonstrate this theory," Rex continued, "some 20 years ago I decided I wanted some edelweiss in the rock garden, so I read up on it: Four articles in my collection of magazines and a chapter in each of three books. Then, feeling that I knew all that man had discovered about edelweiss, I selected a spot, prepared it accordingly, got plants from a good grower, and put the little dears in the ground.

"The following spring no sign of edelweiss, and that identical performance was annually repeated for six years; I checked over and over with the information, to make sure I wasn't slipping up somewhere. The seventh year I was finally rewarded: one wretched little sprig of edelweiss showed up, and, outraged, I lifted it with a trowel and transplanted it in a wet, poorly-drained border that never got much sun, back of some primroses; a place having all of the attributes edelweiss is supposed to hate, and none of those it likes, according to the literature. This was 13 years ago; that spot (about 5 feet square) has gradually become as fine a plantation of healthy and happy edel-

Native Americans fed pumpkins to their horses. Food manufacturers use tan colored pumpkins to make pumpkin puree.

weiss as you would care to see."

I believed every word of this, and when he went on to say he had had similar experiences with blue gentian, trailing arbutus, hybrid columbine, yellow lady slipper, and so on, I flippantly suggested:

"So the answer is simple enough: the way to grow flowering plants successfully is to read the rules, then carefully violate all of them."

Good to know, if true, but we both had to admit that we had successfully grown a great number of plants by following the rules. Rex said he had decided that flowers are like wives; each and every individual one is unique, but he added that with plants, just as with wives, you might as well begin by following the rules (some of them, anyway), provided you know how to interpret them.

"Which reminds me of a zinnia story," he said, "Neil and Sara bought a place in the country and proceeded to garden like crazy. They asked me to dinner the Fourth of July and had a list of horticultural questions ready for me. One of their troubles was that their zinnias hadn't come up, and to prove they had bought good seeds they showed me the empty envelope, and also declared they had carefully followed instructions.

"Sara said: 'For instance, it says on the envelope that the distance should be 12 inches, so we dug the trench exactly 12 inches deep, even measuring it with a ruler.' Before you follow any rule, you do have to understand it." And it doesn't hurt to try figuring out some of your own, I was thinking, but I kept still; Rex would get

Knowledge is knowing a tomato is a fruit; Wisdom is not putting it in a fruit salad.

around to that, I was fairly sure. And he did.

"When the new hybrid petunias began to be available," he said, "all the articles by experts said they should be started in flats, so I did this the first three or four years. And I never had a complete failure, always getting some plants, but never as many as I wanted; the little seedlings took a lot of tending, too.

"Three years ago I decided to try another way: in August I mulched a spot (12 square feet) with salt hay to keep the dirt mellow and to abolish weeds; in November I removed the mulch, lightly loosened the top one-quarter inch of soil, and, after mixing the petunia seed with granulated sugar, I broadcast them over the 12 square feet. No raking in,

"The following spring I got a much higher percentage, having about 220 plants left after three thinnings. I now use this routine with all annuals which self-sow in my climate."

I wanted to ask why, if they self-sow, he doesn't just leave them alone — let them do the whole job themselves. It could be he meant those flowers which he was planting for the first time, or there might be some reason why it's better to plant fresh seeds every year, even if the flower is self-sowing. But I didn't ask any questions; if there is a reason why these plants should have a fresh sowing every year, I don't want to know it. I am busy enough.

Now Rex was off on a different angle: "There are two kinds of gardeners — those who insist on trying to master the demand and temperaments of the more difficult flora, and those who refuse to bother with the prima donnas. The latter gardeners, of whom I am

About 3,500 honey bees fly 55,000 miles to make 1 pound of honey. It takes 10 pounds of nectar to make a pound of honey.

one, fill their beds with friendly types which will stand for a lot of give and take.

"For instance, a friend of mine insists on growing Lady Washington geraniums, because they're more difficult to manage, whereas I have zonals, because they're easier to grow — and just as desirable. My favorite geraniums are the scented-leaved ones; they don't flower as exuberantly as zonals, but the great variety of their fragrances more than compensates. The apple geranium is my particular pet and from October to May I keep four or five of them here and there around the house, rarely passing one without thumbing a leaf and having a sniff."

Then, with a sidelong glance at me, Rex suggested: "What say we end this with controversy?"

"Sure, why not?" I shrugged, but was alert, wondering what was coming.

"For one thing, you're going to make a religion out of gardening, if you don't watch out," he said. "There's nothing wrong with mulch but if you, for instance, pile it thick on Virginia bluebells, you won't get any spread. Organic gardening is okay, but if there's too much organic matter in your nasturtium soil, you'll get only leaves — no flowers. Chemical fertilizers are all right if you know how to use them properly, and can afford them. There's nothing wrong with spraying for insects and diseases if your nose can stand the smell, and your back and pocketbook can stand the strain." He stopped and grinned. "Your turn."

"You sound like a roomful of garden club women," I began.

One green chili has the vitamin C of six oranges.

"About Virginia bluebells: if they won't spread under mulch, skip it. . . . Plant nasturtiums in poor soil but put mulch on top to keep moisture in and weeds out. ... If you're devoted to chemical fertilizer, enjoy yourself; I don't need it. As to poison spraying, I loathe the job and the odor, and can't get rid of the perhaps fanciful notion that maybe the poisons don't discriminate between good and bad bugs; so I don't spray and I never lose a vegetable crop. I have black leaf spots on my roses, but so do people who spray theirs. I wouldn't advise anyone not to spray, that's his affair, but I'm genuinely sorry for sprayers."

I added: "If you were a group of gardeners, I would probably end this way: 'Read what the experts say, if you want to, then go ahead and use your own brains, too, not just theirs.' "

Thinking it over, it's true that Rex has learned two things from me—the advantages of a year-round mulch, and that a little mulching doesn't retard the growth of iris. And I readily admit that I've learned dozens of things from him which have greatly helped me. Since I don't pretend to know much about gardening in general, it's relaxing to realize that if I need some information such as, say, the official name for mountain pink, I can always ask Rex.

GARDEN PESTS—THEY AREN'T SO BAD!

This isn't going to be an attempt to tell you how to get rid of all your little garden enemies, and if you run across such an article, don't be taken in; I doubt if anyone knows. That wonderful creature called

When Sir Walter Raleigh first brought potatoes to the court of Queen Elizabeth I, there seems to have been a lack of communication. The cooks tossed out the tubers, and boiled the stems and leaves. Everyone who partook became deathly ill and potatoes were banned from the Royal kitchen for a long time!

man, who has learned how to make bombs which can wipe out quite a sizable number of his fellow beings with one blast, looks a bit puny when he undertakes to eliminate something the size of a mosquito or aphis and keep it eliminated without getting into trouble of one kind or another.

Woodchucks

Through the years I have had a lot of trouble with woodchucks. Some time ago a friend told me that since soybeans are the favorite food of this animal (which I already knew and I must admit they have good taste, if nothing else), the simple thing was to plant a fence of soybeans all around your garden and the animals would go no further. This sounded perfect to me — not much trouble or expense and such a large growth of the beans would surely satisfy all wood chucks in the vicinity. So I put the seeds in, they came up, then the next thing that happened was so very obvious — afterwards: The clever beasts didn't wait for the beans to get very high; they cleaned up the whole fence (in one night) when the plants had grown about two inches, then went on to lesser but still edible things in the garden.

Well, we next put a chicken-wire fence around the plot and it took no time at all for us to discover that woodchucks are good climbers. So we put more wire at right angles to the top of the fence, but rather loose and floppy, so that when the animal got up that high he was stopped. This was about 5 years ago and the idea seemed to work, and I have been calling attention to it to anyone interested, and have also told about it sometimes when speaking to various groups.

Thomas Jefferson first introduced French Fries to the White House during his presidency. He had been the Ambassador to France during the American Revolution, and had his chef trained in France, where he learned to make them.

However, I discovered one morning early this summer that some animals had gotten inside my patch the night before. I had carefully checked (just as a matter of precaution) the floppy fence a few weeks previously and had thought it was all right; that morning I slowly went over it again and still couldn't find anything wrong, so I consulted John Lorenz—my neighbor, fellow-gardener, and invaluable adviser. The only conclusion he could come to was that a woodchuck had finally figured out how to get over that wobbly roof, as, incidentally, raccoons had done a few years before.

We examined the whole fence again and thought we knew where the woodchuck must have entered; so John made a barricade and set a trap. The next morning he drove in early, went out to the garden, and a few minutes later when he came into the kitchen, there was a broad grin on his face.

"Well, I got Mr. Mastermind," he announced, "and I'll now put two traps outside the fence for any others that aren't so smart."

He caught two more in those traps in the next few days, but of course I can no longer tell anyone that a wire fence with a wobbly roof will defeat woodchucks — not only a wrong conclusion, but also a most uneasy feeling. My first visit to my garden each morning is actually like a trip into the unknown.

Mice and Moles

I have been asked many times whether or not my method attracts rats and mice. I've never seen either in my garden in spring, summer, or fall, and if they tuck themselves in under the hay in win-

---

The British are particularly fond of parsnips. It was British colonists that introduced the vegetable into the New World in 1609. Even the American Indians readily took up the growing of parsnips. In 1779 Gen. John Sullivan in his forays against the Iroquois destroyed stores of parsnips grown by these Indians in western New York.

ter, should I begrudge them such a cozy spot? They can't do any harm at that time of year, and it's better to have them there than in the house.

As for mulching attracting moles and mice to your tulips, well, I've mulched mine all the year round for over twenty years and I haven't lost any bulbs. People do have an awful time keeping these pests from their tulips, but they seem to have just as much trouble when they don't mulch. The only satisfactory solution I've heard of is to plant the bulbs in wire baskets. I'm not sure I would want tulips badly enough to bother with that, since there are so many other lovely flowers around in tulip time.

I used to be pestered every few years with mole runs in my garden but haven't seen any since I started mulching. Two summers ago our lawn was a veritable subway but there wasn't one run in the mulched flower beds, which are right in the yard. Yet I'm forced to believe that the mulching isn't the reason for this, for I know of mulched gardens which have moles. I've had a number of letters reproaching me because mulching attracted moles, and have had just as many from people saying they were grateful to me because their mulching has chased the moles away. So what can we call all of it but coincidence?

Raccoons

Do raccoons or something eat your corn just about when you're planning to enjoy it yourself? I defeat them this way: When a row of corn is about ready to be picked (and that seems to be the time

Okra goes by a myriad of names, according to various world languages. One moniker for the vegetable, stands out, however. "Gombo" or, as many Southerners likely know it "gumbo" is a word commonly used to identify okra. The term originates from the original Spanish-Portuguese word for okra, "quingombo", which is a corruption of the word "quillobo", which describes the region of East Africa.

when the raccoons want it), I prop some old screens and bushel baskets up against the stalks. Since I never have more than a 30 foot row ready to eat at one time this isn't a tremendous job.

Someone laughed at me for doing this (a man, of course — I know that the screen and baskets are a woman's trick), and said that all it meant was that no animal was after my corn. But that wasn't true, because I had done this only after some ears had been eaten. Then I tried propping the screens against all but a few stalks; sure enough, the next morning the exposed stalks were stripped while the others remained intact.

Cutworms

Until last summer I hadn't had one plant ruined by a cutworm during the thirteen-year mulch era although I had formerly had plenty of trouble with them. Then, last June, two of my tomato plants were cut off. I found the offenders and also discovered that those two plants didn't have the hay tucked up closely around them. I took care to see that the others were adequately mulched and didn't lose any more of them.

Slugs

During the past years I have had many letters from gardeners who were having slug trouble — and did I know what to do about this pest? Well, I didn't know; I've never had any slugs, and hadn't heard them discussed very often. Then a friend of mine, Bethany Killgren, telephoned me about two months ago to say that, for the first time,

The first recorded watermelon harvest occurred nearly 5,000 years ago in Egypt. Early explorers used watermelons as canteens.

her plants were being attacked by slugs.

Suddenly I remembered that I had once heard (but this was told in a rather joking way) that if you set a pan of beer out in your garden overnight, next morning the container will be full of slugs, either dead or dead drunk. At any rate, they will have had it.

I told Bethany about the beer routine, and the next day she called me and in a thrilled tone said she had put out the beer, and that it really worked. So I wrote up her success in my weekly column in 3 Connecticut papers, and she and I soon began to get telephone calls from excited and delighted gardeners who were trying the beer treatment.

A few weeks later, when the town of Redding had a bicentennial celebration—its 200th year as a town— one day was given over to exhibiting several gardens, and I was asked to be a guest. Well, many of the people there spoke to me about their experiments with the slug-beer routine after having read my column. One of the show gardens even had, as a sort of display, a row of pans of beer, filled with dead slugs. Then a man came up to me to report that he had counted the casualties in his garden—1,000 slugs in 3 days.

Borers

I read an article a year or so ago about how to defeat the squash borer. I tried it and it works. When my Hubbard squash vine was a few feet long, I pulled the mulch from under it at one spot, saw to it that the vine touched the dirt right there and covered the vine with hay in that one place. It took root there, and as the vine grew, I

Strawberries do not ripen after picking.

did this a few more times. The borers got into the hill where I had planted the seed and that part of the vine died, but the rest of it lived, since it had become rooted along the vine. I had fine squash.

In twenty-five years of gardening I had never seen a corn borer and perhaps not more than a dozen ear worms. Then my book came out, saying this, and the next year there was a worm in every ear of my corn. Moral: don't write a book. That was several seasons ago. Last summer there wasn't one single ear worm in my corn.

Now the significant thing about those beetle and ear worm stories is this: I guess we've all heard that we should burn every diseased plant, and, whatever we do, we shouldn't leave them in the garden. Well, I didn't remove those infested bean vines and corn stalks, since the keynote of my activities seems to be: "I wonder?" Or, less elegantly, "Oh yeah?" And sure enough, in spite of my disobedience to the rules, not a beetle and not an earworm did I have the following season!

I have also read that all the old asparagus should be burned in the fall, to guard against disease. I not only don't burn mine, I don't even cut it. By spring it has died a natural death and I leave it in the garden for mulch. My old bed of asparagus, which hasn't been given a thing but hay for many years, is to put it modestly, satisfactory.

As to some of the other unwanted comers into your garden— in other words, pests—may I suggest that you don't get unduly upset about them? A woman who was wearing glasses, and who came here to have a look at my mulched garden, went on at great length about the various kinds of bugs she had seen on her plants, although she

One bushel of corn will sweeten more than 400 cans of Coca-Cola.

didn't seem to be at all sure that they were doing any damage.

Finally I said: "May I give you a little advice? Leave your glasses in the house wherever you go out to your garden."

There are two things I've learned about pests. One is not to believe everything I hear or read about them. The other is that however generously they may help themselves to the product of my labor, as a rule they courteously leave quite a bit for me.

CHAPTER 3.

Beauty With a Bow

HERE'S WHAT MY OWN flower beds would look like if you should pay me a visit. In the first place, starting as you enter the driveway there is a large triangular bed of mountain pink, and the only attention of any kind this gets is admiration (in spring, of course) from callers and from cars passing by, which often slow up to get a better look. Next, as you drive a little farther in, you will see, on your left, a space partly covered with myrtle. And only partly, because I started the bed with a dozen small plants some years ago and slowly but

Broccoli is a member of the Brassicaceae family which also includes cabbage, kale, and cauliflower. All are descended from the same plant.

surely it is making its way out to the driveway.

As it creeps along, I keep the grass in its wide path covered with mulch so that the myrtle will have nothing to combat on its way. Also, the leaves which fall over the bed in autumn are left there; I used to carefully rake them off in spring with my hands, but that isn't only unnecessary (for they soon disappear) but it is too bad, since removing the leaves deprived the myrtle of good nourishment.

At the starting point of the myrtle, opposite the kitchen door, is a large, droopy bridal wreath bush which my mother planted there thirty years ago, when it was a mere sprig. For some time I kept it mulched, but the myrtle has crept all around it, so it now gets only the leaves which blow and stop there.

Under the kitchen windows are bushes of single peonies always deeply mulched by their own tops, which I never cut off, and by the leaves which blow up against the house. Close by, under the pantry window and in line with the peonies, is a New Dawn climbing rose.

In front of all this is a row of columbine, and here and there are some single asters, which do well in this spot because they like semi-shade. This year I also put in a few verbenas here, to add to the general gaiety. All of this is heavily mulched with hay and leaves, but, to fool my public, I cover the mulch with a liberal sprinkling of rich dirt (compost to you) from the vegetable garden. Sometimes a visitor will say: "Oh, so you don't mulch your flower beds!" Then I invite them to look under the dirt.

There are other ways to "beautify" the background of flower

Lima beans have been grown in Peru for the past 9,000 years. It is named after Peru's capital, Lima. The plant's proper name, "lunatus," means "half-moon" and refers to the shape of the bean. Potatoes, quinoa, and lima beans were staple products during the Incan empire in the Andes region.

beds; you can chop the hay and leaves, or use buckwheat hulls, or peat moss, or any of the other commodities which you may like better than hay. Sometimes I use nearly-rotted mulch.

Before I go any further, I'll explain why I have so many separate flower beds. I don't like objets d'art, I don't care how beautiful, crowded together on a mantel place; museums tire me; flower shows wear me out. And, if a flower bed has more than one kind of flower in it, I want them to have some relation to each other, choosing them with as much care as I'd choose a hat to go with my gown, providing I ever wore a hat— which I don't.

A few feet in front of the columbine and aster bed is a triangle of petunias and rose moss (portulaca). In April this spot was practically sensational; it was covered with crocuses and glory-of-the-snow and scilla. Actually, I never get caught bragging about my ability to grow flowers because I haven't much, but for some reason crocuses like to put themselves out for me.

Many years ago I started that crocus bed by just sticking in a few bulbs in one end of it. They were yellow, white and lavender, and I'm sure there weren't more than a dozen bulbs altogether, but now they not only come up in huge clusters but they have also hopped around all over the bed. And I defy the most artistic landscape expert to do as good a job as the crocuses themselves have done. By the time they finish blooming, the leaves have become so thick and long that I have to knot them together, so that the petunias and rose moss will have a chance. This bed, as you can see, has only low-growing flowers and is a riot of color.

Beets were considered an aphrodisiac in ancient Roman times. Modern scientists have found that beets absorb and store high amounts of boron, which is essential in creating human sex hormones.

Across the stone walk by this bed is a long row of tulips which I haven't dug up for many years. They are still doing fine, and, to take the curse off the dying tops, there are California poppies in this bed which seed themselves. Therefore, this space and the petunia bed must have the mulch pushed back temporarily in order to give the seeds a chance to germinate. Then the plants always come up too thick, but an excellent and quick way to thin them is to just put some mulch on the ones you don't want. In May I plant zinnia seeds one foot apart along the tulip row; they furnish color when the poppies begin to get bored.

All of my bulbs are, of course, constantly mulched all year round. One of my favorite people is a woman in Michigan, (or maybe it's Wisconsin), who wrote me that she had cancelled her subscription to a well-known garden magazine because they had published an article which said that the mulch should be removed from bulbs at some time or other (I've forgotten when and why), Her point was that they had published an article by me sometime before, in which I said the opposite, so the magazine should of course have known better. How's that for faith?

On the other side of the petunia bed is a frog pond edged by blue iris, lilies-of-the-valley, sedum — all mulched, of course. Around this is a white fence, and just inside it and hanging over it, is a row of peony bushes, heavy with blossoms every season. The last two years I planted some Little Sweetheart sweet peas, cosmos, bachelor's-buttons and a few Heavenly Blue morning-glories along the outside of the fence. I like tall flowers against the fence and I love the morning-

Betanin, which is derived from beetroots, is used to color tomato paste, sauces, candy, breakfast cereals, ice cream, jams, and jellies.[

glories creeping along it, making an attractive combination.

Along the driveway are three thriving holly bushes, a Rosa hugonis bush, and a couple of hybrid teas. These latter are handicapped by tree roots from a big maple, and the first person who acts as though he would like to have these bushes will get them. I have exerted myself, mentally and physically, in the effort to make the space between these bushes attractive because this section is the first thing the eye falls on when one drives in.

Last year I planted verbenas all along the row, and at the end farthest from the maple tree the plants thrived. But the tree roots obviously interfered along the rest of the row. I think I now have this licked, though, and in the following way: Each year I have the man from whom I buy tomato plants start my lobelia, and there are many dozens of them; I formerly used them as a border around most of the flower beds. But this year I transplanted all of them into a number of flats, and I have put these in a row between the holly and tea roses. Then I mulched all around them and put some dirt on top, so they look as if they are planted in the ground. The tree roots can't disturb them and they will be easy to water, if necessary. How do I know this will work? Because last year I didn't get around to putting all of the lobelia in the flower beds, and those I left in the flat, although much too close together, outshone all others.

I will, however, again put verbenas at the far end of the row; then, on the other side of the Rosa hugonis I have planted a few branching asters and also some single ones, plus a trellis of morning glories.

Babe Ruth used to wear a cabbage leaf under his hat during games. He would switch out for a fresh leaf halfway through each game.

My pet bed is near one end of the tulip row: annual phlox. I've had a difficult time with these the last few seasons, so this year I started them indoors in jiffy pots. When I ordered the seeds and pots and told the supplier what I was going to do, he wrote back that for a woman who admittedly tried to save work, I was going to an awful lot of trouble for some phlox. But I found that it actually was less work than planting the seed in the bed. Doing it that way, I first had to pull away all mulch and leave it off for quite awhile; then, when the plants showed up, I had to thin them, which is quite a job. And when they were big enough, I had to mulch the bed again, otherwise there would have been weeding and cultivating and watering to be done all summer.

So, this year, in March, when one can't do much outside any-way, I mixed some dirt with vermiculite and filled the tiny pots, dropped a few of the phlox seeds in each one, covered them with sphagnum moss, put the pots in some flats, and set them in a warm place. As soon as the seeds germinated, I put them outdoors to harden, but of course I had to bring them inside some nights.

The thing to do is to leave only one plant in a pot. Some of the plants looked so healthy and strong that I carefully pulled them out and made an extra bed; and since they were so small, they thrived. However, for the section of phlox which I had originally planned on, I had enough plants in pots. All I had to do when the time came was to take a trowel and put them in the bed, six inches apart, without hav-ing to disturb the mulch. A very much easier and quicker process than planting the seeds in the ground.

Chik-fil-A sent the creator of a popular "Eat More Kale" shirt, Bo Muller-Moore, a cease-and-desist letter in 2011, saying that "Eat More Kale" was too much like the fast food company's own slogan, "Eat More Chikin." The U.S. Patent and Trademark Office allowed Muller-Moore to trademark his kale boosterism in 2014.

This bed is my favorite because of the colors, I suppose, which include everything but the yellow shades. Also, the designs are varied and lovely. It is startling but never brash. How anything can contrive to look so conspicuously beautiful and yet modest, I will never know. And they keep right on blooming through a few frosts. So do verbena which I also especially love.

In the yard opposite the barn is a flowering crab, and another bed of peonies in which I also put some asparagus roots this year. And just beyond that, the driveway turns around a large bed of iris, which is heavily mulched and doing beautifully in spite of the experts' idea that you mustn't mulch this flower. Onions and potatoes are planted all around the edge of the iris bed; they come up through the hay.

You may ask: why do I do this? Well, there's all that nice space in which I was going to plant day lilies and didn't. When the iris have called it a day, the potatoes show up, fresh and eager, looking better than the iris at this point. So—why not?
And if anyone thinks he wouldn't care for this last plebeian item, he doesn't have to drive in and around the iris bed; he can leave his car in the road.

GARDENIAS I HAVE KNOWN

Not long ago I offered a begonia plant to a man who had come to my place from Long Island to talk about gardening, and he said; "No, thanks, they are too easy to grow. But if you have a small garde-

Researchers at the USDA found that study participants who consumed 2 carrots a day were able to lower their cholesterol levels about 20 percent due to a soluble fibre called calcium pectate.

nia plant that you could give me, that would be fine, I like something difficult to do—then I can boast about it if I succeed."

I replied: "Then you don't want a gardenia. I know of no house plant that is easier to grow."

It is really a little sad to think of the way people have been misled about gardenias. Yes, here I go-sounding off again about the so-called authorities. Some of my friends and acquaintances, who know of my success with this supposedly difficult plant, send me articles now and then, which say in effect that it is practically impossible to grow a gardenia in an "ordinary household." And the piece invariably goes on to say that if you are determined to try, you should keep the plant in the sun all day. Instructions are also invariably given about keeping the soil wet—but none of the choices of the way to do that are ever as simple as the obvious one of sitting the flower pot in a pan which has water in it! Too, these "experts" nearly always assure you that mealy bugs will almost certainly show up, so you must spray the plant often. And when (not if) this doesn't kill the pests, try swabbing them.

Many of those articles are written by people I never heard of, but the first one I remember seeing, about 16 years ago, in the *New York Herald Tribune*, was by Mr. Connors of Rutgers University. And one of the latest ones I read was also in a New York newspaper, on a garden page which is conducted by a Mr. Everett, who is, I believe, a well-known writer about gardening. His information about gardenias was given to a woman, in answer to her complaint that her plant was turning yellow, the buds were dropping off, and she seemed very

There are two competing theories as to where cauliflower came from. The French are convinced its roots lay in Cyprus. For this reason they once called it choux de Chypre, meaning Cyprus cabbages. Of course, those from Cyprus take credit for the cauliflower's existence and introduction into our diets.

anxious to save it. He gave her the usual sun- exposure, vague-watering routine (careful, not very wet) adding that nothing would probably work, and I, feeling sorry for the woman, wrote to Mr. Everett for her address, telling him that I had good news for her.

Well, I got a reply from him, which was more than I had had from Mr. Connors when I wrote to him, years before, in regard to his article. Mr. Everett said that he knew about my claims about gardenias, but that he didn't agree with me. About a week later I again wrote him, to thank him for a lobster dinner I had just enjoyed. I had made a bet with a friend that either Mr, Everett wouldn't answer me at all, or—if he did—that he wouldn't give me the woman's address. And he didn't.

More than 30 years ago a friend gave me a small gardenia plant, and told me to let it have only a little sun, to water it generously every day, and also to keep it sitting in a pan of water. And for nourishment, just to put back into the pot any leaves that dropped off, along with the old blossoms when they were removed. And he advised repotting the plant, of course, when it became big enough to require it.

Well, my gardenia thrived. It got bigger and bigger and bloomed luxuriously. And although I had always felt that I had no talent for starting a plant from cuttings, I couldn't resist trying it, because so many of my friends were eager for a gardenia. But I couldn't have been more casual about this—simply clipping off a sprig and sticking it in a small pot of dirt from my mulched garden. Of course, I kept the soil in the little pots very wet.

Not a fan of the way cauliflower smells when you boil it? Try adding celery seeds or celery leaves to the water. It's a simple way to cut down the smell.

Each month of the year I started a gardenia slip, to try to find out when the best time was to do it. Those potted in spring seemed to prosper more than the others. However, I didn't make enough tests to say this with real conviction. During the summer, the original plant and all the young cuttings were kept out of doors in virtual shade. Some years ago, when the 4 professors from Storrs Agricultural College came to have a first hand look at my garden, my gardenia plant was over 5 feet tall and covered with buds and blossoms. It had, for the first time, too much yellow in its leaves. One of the men said to give it iron, and told me what to buy, and I did, but have forgotten what the product was. Anyway, it worked; the leaves soon returned to normal. One day, a little later, it occurred to me that there might be a simpler way to feed iron to the gardenia plant. I scouted around and found a few rusty nails and stuck them into the soil, and the yellow has never returned to the leaves. But whether or not that's due to the nails is a moot question.

Now, almost any "authority" on plants — who either thinks he knows all about them, or at least isn't going to admit that he doesn't — would probably contend that my experience is an exception, perhaps because my "ordinary household" happens to be one that has enough humidity to keep a plant healthy. Well, in the first place, I have a hot-air furnace, besides which — and much more convincing — I have also given at least a hundred small slips to friends and acquaintances and have been able to check enough of the plants to know that they are, almost without exception, thriving.

Or it might be said that since those slips were all taken from

The first garden strawberry was grown in Brittany, France, during the late 18th century. Prior to this, wild strawberries and cultivated selections from wild strawberry species were the common source of the fruit. The strawberry fruit was mentioned in ancient Roman literature in reference to its medicinal use.

the same plant, that it may be exceptional in some mysterious way. But no, for what about this: Now and then some defeated person has brought me a gardenia plant, which he has been given or has bought, and it is obviously about to call it a day—but it is brought back and is soon thriving, if the plant just gets very little sun and the dirt is kept wet.

There is, of course, the sort of person who simply can't leave a plant alone. When I talked to a garden club group some months ago, one of the women, during the question period, said she had read my garden book, had carefully followed my instructions about gardenias, and her plant had done very well for several months. But now it had begun to drop its buds, and she was afraid it was done for. Well, having learned quite a little in recent years about people's attitude toward growing things, I didn't ask her if she had been feeding it anything; I said: "What have you been feeding it?" and she replied, "Well you know, I first tried so-and-so, and then I. . . ." And so on. I told her: "If you will again read what I said about this plant, you will see that you haven't followed instructions; to the soil of my gardenia I add only its own dead leaves and its discarded blossoms." Surely, plants—like children— can only be harmed by overcoddling.

Speaking of the leaves of a gardenia turning brown and dying, I have found that when my plant is brought back into the house in the fall, a certain number of the leaves do this, which seems to be a normal procedure; that is, something like trees and bushes shedding their foliage, although of course the gardenia doesn't lose all of its leaves. In fact, hardly enough of them drop off to notice that any are

Though collard greens did not originate in Africa but originated in the eastern Mediterranean, it wasn't until the first Africans arrived in Jamestown, Virginia in the early 1600s that America got its first taste of the dark green, leafy vegetable.

gone.

When I give away cuttings, I have always kept an extra one, for fear my big plant might decide to give up some day—which it finally did over 10 years ago. After it was brought into the house at the end of that summer, it soon began to look sick and then "worser." The friend who had given it to me, and who knew much more about gardenias than I ever will, could find no reason for such behavior. He finally decided that the plant had had it, and he was sure it was finished— apparently a casualty of old age.

So I was faced with a dilemma: Could a person who had held forth to the extent I had in regard to the care of a gardenia plant admit that hers had died and she didn't really know why? Obviously not, so after giving the matter a little thought, I decided to banish the plant to the porch, and just say that it froze. And I did have it put there, but either my honesty—or perhaps pride in thinking up such a good "out" for both the plant and me—took over and I spilled the whole story, regardless, to anyone interested.
I now had only one small plant, but one of my friends asked me, as a favor, to exchange it for the gardenia I had started for her some years back, because hers had really become too large for her living room. So we traded, and I again had a plant which was taller than I am and broader—even with my arms extended.

This past spring I decided to keep count of the gardenia blossoms as I picked them (either to give to someone or to put back into the pot), but when the number had reached 175, I got bored with keeping track and quit. More than that, I really got fed up with hav-

An essential oil obtained from the fruits and leaves of the dill plant, is used not only for pickles, but also in chewing gums and candy. One tablespoon of dill seed contains more calcium than a cup of milk.

ing another such huge plant around. Thousands of visitors have come here to see my mulched garden, and they, of course, notice the gardenia and carry on about it — and enough is too much, sometimes. A friend of mine, who loves coffee, doesn't have it every day, because she feels that any food or drink, no matter how much you like it, is definitely enjoyed more if it is indulged in only now and then.

The above attitude makes sense to me, and an enormous plant (which requires two men to move it) in your home is certainly a constant thing. So the only solution to the question of the gardenia's perpetual presence that I could come up with was to give it away. Which I did.

SOME FLOWERS I LOVE

Lilacs were the first thing I planted here on Poverty Hollow Farm years ago. With a trowel I dug up some small sprouts from an old bush and stuck them into the ground. That isn't, Tm afraid, the best way to plant a lilac; it surely needs a decent-sized hole.
A few years later I put some larger bushes into bigger holes, and, as time went on, I travelled from one theory to another: I cut off all old blossoms, did some pruning, clipped off young shoots, added fertilizer now and then, including manure. Then I abandoned all this loving care, and as far as I can see, this has made no difference in the health of the bushes.

About 15 years ago I was told that lilacs like wood ashes and I was delighted to hear this, for I had, in an effort to get rid of mine,

Cranberries, Concord grapes, and blueberries are three popular fruits native to North America.

been making my vegetable- garden soil too alkaline, at least, I was told that. So I dumped ashes on the lilac bushes all winter, and when spring came we had more blossoms than ever before, and finer ones. Conclusion: wood ashes are wonderful for lilacs. Then I learned it was a very good lilac year, that everyone around had a profusion and extra lovely blossoms. Moral: be wary of conclusions.

Crocuses and March—strange bedfellows! If anything ever conquered violence and harshness with serenity and indifference, these gallant little flowers do it; they smile at blizzards and shrug their shoulders at frost and snow. But they need protection against that other gentle creature, the rabbit, who likes to nibble their early, welcome green; you can help by bending a long piece of hardware cloth into a tent and putting it over the small plants.

Your tulips and crocuses (as well as the rest of your garden) have, I hope, been under a thick mulch all winter. Now the tulips come pushing through, and before very long we have a great show of gaiety. In spite of the experts my row of tulips has thrived in the same spot for over ten years—never dug up, mulch never removed. And no fertilizer is needed except the constantly-rotting hay and leaves.

In the same row, California poppies seed themselves, and in a nearby bed, rose moss (or portulaca) does the same. Such flowers require a little special attention in a mulched garden: the small plants can't come through much mulch, so I pull it to the edge of the bed. Soon, many more plants than you need will appear, but instead of thinning them, all you have to do is put some mulch on top of many of them, leaving exposed only enough to fill the bed.

Fig flowers are carnivorous - they trap and digest the wasps that pollinate them.

There is something endearing about rose moss; it seems to be a favorite with everyone. But it has one grave fault: it takes naps and its favorite time for doing this is just as visitors arrive.

California poppies, delicately-lovely but rugged, bloom quite early and then on for weeks. After sort of half-resting for awhile, the poppies pick up again to ward fall and bloom profusely even through a few, light frosts.

We have a lot of peonies and they require no work at all, unless you consider picking them to be work. For one thing, the leaves from nearby trees fall on them, or are blown to them and get caught underneath and stay forever, as mulch. Also, the tops of the peony plants are left right there in the garden, to enrich the soil. Many of the people who have come to inspect my method of growing things are surprised at the latter; they believe what they have been told—that the tops of the plants must be cut off in the fall and burned. This I have never done, and we could scarcely have more satisfactory peonies.

If I was obliged to name my favorite flower. I would be tempted to say; a large single white peony. Bigness in other flowers— such as dahlias, zinnias, roses— doesn't impress me, but this particular white peony (with a yellow center) is so fragile-looking and exquisite that its size somehow adds to its beauty. It is faintly, but delightfully, fragrant, and if you should touch one of its petals you would find it to be softer than the finest velvet.

It was years before I attempted to pick any of these peonies for a bouquet; I had the feeling that they wouldn't last in a vase. But they

Soil with lots of worms in it doesn't flood easily after heavy rain because the water drains away thanks to all the worm holes.

do—they stay fresh for days, and I have also discovered that I can mail them, in bud, to New York, with complete success. The next time I live I wish I might be a single, white peony so that people would (as I have so often seen them do) involuntarily catch their breath at sight of me.

We grow some Heavenly Blue morning-glories each year on a high trellis; we would miss that lovely mass of color which often has a matching sky for a background. Ever since I read that one should plant this flower in small pots and transplant it with the ball of dirt around it, I have religiously done this.

But last summer, after the potted ones were put out and not doing very well (it had been miserably cold, and then too hot, for June), I planted the left-over seeds along the white fence which Fred put up to keep his turtles from running away. These seeds grew and finally produced as plentifully as the potted plants did. Learn as you go. But don't be too sure of what you've learned.

Have you ever grown a cypress vine? Its foliage is dainty and attractive and it has small red and white star-shaped flowers. I had one last summer, along the fence by the morning-glories; then came some nasturtiums, handy to the house. If you wanted something fresh and green to add to a sandwich, you didn't have to go out to the garden for lettuce; you could just step outside and grab a nasturtium leaf or two.

Thunbergia. I can't say this is exactly a favorite of mine, but it's a pleasant sort of plant (or vine, really) with a dark-centered yellow flower. If you have a bed of roses you will surely want to keep them

The word "peach" is from the Latin malum Persicum, which literally means "Persian apple."

under constant mulch (to defeat weeds, hold in moisture, enrich the soil) and thunbergia makes an attractive cover for this mulch. Put in the seeds, or small plants, a foot apart; the vine will spread and cover the ground, it won't use too much nourishment or moisture if you have plenty of hay and leaves underneath, and it is prettier than peat moss, for instance.

In passing I will say just one thing about roses: if, in October, you read that they should be planted in the fall, don't make a big effort to do this. For in the spring the same people will, in order to make sales, be telling you: NOW is the time to plant roses.

I always grow a few single asters because of their delightful colors. And, also, they bloom until quite late.

If you want to be sure of at least one prospering flower in your yard, regardless of the weather or anything else, grow some petunias. There are many pretty varieties and a more cooperative flower I have never seen.

Now a few words about house plants. I have already written so much about gardenias, defying the experts right and left, that here I will just put it all into one sentence: keep your plant out of the sun and water it plentifully every day.

When Fred, my husband, gave me a large and expensive amaryllis bulb years ago, I thought with dismay: I probably won't have any luck with that. But, carefully following directions, I potted it and some green soon began to show. The leaves grew rapidly, and, finally, there were six gorgeous blossoms.

During the summer, I put the plant outdoors, kept it watered, and brought it in before frost. I hadn't fed it anything, which was the only rule I ignored. In October I stopped watering it; then, in January I removed the bulb, replaced the soil with fresh rich earth (rotted mulch from the garden), put the bulb back into the pot and began to water it. It made four blossoms this time, so amaryllis-growing isn't, apparently, very difficult.

If you want something cheerful around, day in, day out, hang an oxalis in a sunny window.

In my garden book I boasted that at last I could grow sweet-peas successfully. Simply mulch them. Then, for two springs mine froze and I complained about that in a column I write for some weekly papers. A man wrote and told me to start them in the fall, so I planted some in late September, and told about this, also, in my col-umn. Shortly after the second column appeared, another man wrote me that fall planting of sweetpeas is all wrong.

I have seen the exceptional ones grown by the man who plants them in the fall, but this morning (I am writing this in November) I went out to inspect my small plants and found them looking dejected and a little reproachful.

I grew up with sweetpeas and am devoted to them, but per-haps the practical thing for me to do is to have a psychiatrist try to re-lieve me of my grim determination to grow them.

DON'T KID AROUND ABOUT ROSES

I suppose it is accurate to say that roses are in a class by them-selves in the flower kingdom, although it is certainly true that they

According to Sir Francis Bacon, gardens are the "purest of human pleasures."

are not everybody's favorite. Most of us hke them, though; many of us love them, and it seems that almost everyone who grows flowers would like to have a rosebush or two.

Then why not? Well, in the past year visitors to our garden almost universally said this about roses: "I love them, but they are so much work and even after I kill myself for them they aren't very satisfactory." Just the other day a visitor said that to me and I pinned her down:

"What makes them so much work? What do you feel you are required to do?"

"The weeding is a never-ending job, but spraying is the worst."

"What is it you spray for?"

"Black leaf spot."

"Does that get rid of it?"

"No, that's the trouble. I still have it."

I had asked dozens of rose growers, some of them excellent gardeners, this question and had always received that answer.

"Then why do you spray?" I asked her.

She looked a little amazed.

"All the books tell you to."

"Yes—but if it doesn't help?"

I told her that I never sprayed my roses and that I had some black leaf spot, but no more than any roses I had ever seen which were conscientiously sprayed. I had given up spraying from discouragement and dis taste for the job and had continued the practice of no

There is a garden in England called The Poison Garden. It is home to 100 murderous plants. Visitors to this dangerous garden are prohibited from smelling, touching, or tasting any of the plants.

spraying from just every day common sense. If the spraying didn't do what it was supposed to do, what was the purpose of my antics? I have one climbing rose, New Dawn, one Rose Hugonis, and 12 hybrid teas. Three of these, a Peace, a Radiance, and a lovely one my mother planted more than 25 years ago whose name I don't know, are at the three corners of the portulaca bed. The others are along the driveway, with three holly bushes in line with them and the Rose Hugonis at one end. The New Dawn is against the house.

I never spray any of these, never weed or fertilize them. They are very, very little work. In the autumn I cover the entire row with five or six inches of hay and leaves. In November I take dirt from between the rows of asparagus and heap some around each hybrid tea rose bush.

This dirt is extremely rich. It is actually compost, for it is simply rotted mulch. I could take it from any place in the vegetable garden, because the entire garden, with its year-round mulch of hay and leaves, is rich compost. But there, between the asparagus rows, this excellent dirt is not needed, and there will always be more.

In the spring this earth which has been heaped up around the roses is judiciously pulled back thinly over the deep mulch. This is the easiest way to dispose of it and also it makes the row of roses look as neat as if there was nothing there but dirt.

If there isn't quite enough earth to cover the hay adequately, all I have to do is bring a few wheelbarrow loads of partly rotted mulch from the garden. Now I have an adequately mulched bed of roses, whose appearance deflates the most critical garden club visitor

Dandelions were used as a food source and as a medicine for at least 1,000 years. European immigrants purposely carried seeds to America, where greens were used for salads and teas. Dandelion roots were served as a vegetable course, or were dried and used as a coffee substitute.

who has come to have a look and ask me to talk to her club, providing my flower beds don't look too awful.

This mulch keeps down weeds, conserves moisture, rots and feeds the roses. The dirt spread thinly on top of it, even if full of weed seeds, will not give me any bothersome weeds, because the tiny ones which start send their roots into hay full of air pockets, and make no headway. They will certainly never rob the roses of any nourishment, but they aren't pretty and so, two or three times a summer, I either pull them out or toss a lot of rotted mulch on them. This probably takes about three hours a season.

I've seen sub-zero roses advertised during the past few years. These are supposed to be immune from winter killing, which doesn't particularly interest me for we always have some sub-zero weather and yet I have lost only one rose—Gray Pearl. More important to me, some sub-zero roses are said to be almost immune to black leaf spot. I have three of them, but haven't had them long enough to know whether this is a fairy tale or not.

New Dawn, Rose Hugonis and Radiance have almost no black leaf spot. I planted my Rose Hugonis— a shrub rose—two years ago and I do wish you could have seen it this spring and wish I had taken a picture of it. It is a beautiful, surprisingly large bush and had hundreds—maybe a thousand or so—dainty, single, yellow blossoms. In these two years it has made three new bushes which I have dug up and given away.

Radiance, a hybrid tea, is a marvelously cooperative rose. It has more blossoms, and blooms more continuously, than any variety

According to one study, as little as 30 minutes of gardening can dramatically improve a man's sex life. Weeding, digging, or mowing the lawn for 30 minutes almost halved a man's risk of impotence.

I am familiar with. It is not sensationally beautiful—just a pretty, friendly, pink rose.

Now, do my bushes have a beautiful supply of roses all summer and fall? No. Do anybody's? I don't think so.

It seems to me that our attitude to hybrid tea roses is too much like our attitude to our friends: we are likely to expect too much of them. If we like half-a- dozen things about a person, why do we feel that he should have a dozen, or even eight, things for us to like? If he is a pleasant addition to a dinner party why must he also be the kind of person who arrives on time?

And so with roses. Just because the people who sell them like to say they are ever blooming, do we have to expect it of them? Because people sell sprays to do away with black leaf spot, do we have to keep on using it when we find that it doesn't do away with it? If you are ambitious enough to read books and articles on roses you will be told over and over that they need a great deal of water. Last fall, after the floods and downpours here in Connecticut, our roses bloomed as never before. Even better than in spring. Peace had fifteen large and lovely blossoms at one time; Radiance had forty. All the roses kept it up until after several light frosts. If I had doubted it before, I knew then that roses like lots of water.

But this is a discouraging thing for many of us. In a dry season everything needs watering but if you have a dug well which may go dry, as many of us have, you can't spare water for your roses. Mulching, of course, is particularly valuable in a dry season, if you are short of water. And yet even watering them plentifully apparently

"Fruit" is a botanical term, while "vegetable" is a culinary term.

doesn't give you the "ever blooming" ones.

We had a neighbor some years ago who went in for roses in a big way. He had plenty of water, lots of money, and was an efficient gardener. He followed all the rules and yet his roses didn't look any better than ours did through the summer months.

What is the answer for us who like roses and would like to grow some? As far as the work is concerned, I mulch them and never have to bother with weeds. I let the rotting hay nourish them and don't have to fool around with manure or fertilizer. I eliminate spraying, since it doesn't get me anywhere. When the professors of agriculture visited my garden one of them said that it was definitely true that healthy plants are less likely to be attacked by bugs than unhealthy ones. Perhaps the kind of food I give my roses keeps them healthy.

Another thing: I have learned to be realistic. I have stopped expecting more from roses than I am likely to get. Just because people who sell roses enjoy calling them "ever blooming," does that mean that I am obliged to believe them?

We don't expect peonies or lilacs to bloom straight through to frost and we are not likely to expect them to until someone gets the bright idea to advertise them as ever blooming. Then what a dither we'll be in, feeling as frustrated over lilacs as we now are over roses! I am happy and satisfied with many lovely roses in June, a spattering through the summer, and a few to pick after some light frosts. The bushes begin to look a bit rocky, it is true, but how do most flowers (and most people, for that matter) look toward the end of their natu-

The Gympie-Gympie tree is the world's most dangerous tree and the most painful of all stinging plant trees. Touching this tree is similar to being sprayed with hot acid, even driving those who have been affected to suicide. One man shot himself after he mistakenly used the leaf as toilet paper.

ral lives?

Is it the fault of the roses that we want more from them than they have to give? Someone said to me. "I like iris, because when they're through they're through. They don't try to kid you." True enough,—and roses don't try to kid us either. But we do seem to be bent on kidding ourselves.

The daffodil's name is from the Old English, affo dyle, or "that which cometh early," because it is one of the earliest blooming flowers.

CHAPTER 4.

The Test Is in the Tasting

A BRIGHT THOUGHT ABOUT EATING VEGETABLES

THE BRIGHT THOUGHT CAME to me one day, many years ago, that if everybody ate his food raw, kitchens could be dispensed with, there would be a big saving in time and labor; also, people could not only discard their stoves, but wouldn't have to buy pots, pans and all that sort of thing. So, for about a year I ate only raw food, and I probably couldn't have done it more unscientifically.

At that time my sister was doing the shopping and cooking for our family, and I told her of my project, but added that she mustn't ever buy any special food for me—that is, something just because it could be eaten raw. I told her that my whole idea was to prove how much simpler hfe would be if no cooking had to be done, and that she mustn't have my diet on her mind at all.

She took me at my word, and the result was that sometimes there was nothing more enticing for me to eat than, say, a raw beet.

There are over 20,000 species of edible plants in the world. However, just 20 species provide 90% of human food.

When I was asked to a friend's home for a meal, I would take perhaps a banana and carrot with me, and I carried my lunch to work each day, usually settling for raisins and whole wheat. My point is that for a year I paid no attention to a balanced diet—and my health remained intact. Moreover, as far as I can remember, I neither gained nor lost weight. This doesn't prove, of course, that a raw-food diet is beneficial, but is, I should think an indication that it isn't harmful.

About flavor: could anything be more fatuous than to try to persuade someone that this or that food has a good taste if he thinks it hasn't? However, I have heard more than one person say that he doesn't like a certain food, and then it comes to light that he has never tasted it. Therefore, may I suggest that before you turn up your nose at the idea of eating, say, a raw potato, you try one?

In March I dig parsnips out of the ground in my garden and for every 3 or 4 I cook, I eat at least one raw. They aren't crisp, like a carrot, but are sweeter. The next thing in the spring that is available is dandelion plants, without anyone needing to give a thought to them. The other day, when I was making a salad of some, the young man who had come to read our meter stopped in my kitchen a moment, and watching me, said: "I have never eaten dandelions raw. My mother always cooks them." I replied that I like them cooked, too, but that one has to pick such a great lot of them to make a meal.

Before the dandelions become old and bitter, asparagus starts to shoot up, and some of the spears, raw or cooked, are a real addition to a salad. In my opinion, asparagus, like corn, is at its flavor peak immediately after being picked, and I often eat a few on the way

The Old English word geard means "fence" and produced the words "garden" and "yard."

from the garden to the kitchen.

All winter long and well into spring I eat Sweet Spanish onions, preferably raw. Perhaps you don't know that these are grown from plants (not sets), and I get mine from Joseph Harris & Co., Rochester, N.Y. The onions which I grow from sets I use for cooking, and when they are scallions I eat them raw. Also, through the winter I dig carrots which I have left out in my garden under bales of hay; these are crisper and sweeter than any you can buy, or even those stored in a root cellar. And this is one vegetable which many people (mostly men and children) like raw and dishke when cooked.

Shall we have a look into the matter of drinking vegetables instead of eating them — that is, making them into a juice? When I recently talked to a group of people in New Hampshire, one woman asked me if the pulp of carrots which had been put through a juicer was as good for mulch as hay. Even though I've heard quite a lot about the frantic activity of juicing things nowadays, I was a bit startled to hear that anyone had enough residue from that project to take the place of hay. I told this woman that there surely wouldn't be enough of the pulp to go very far, but she replied that there were 5 children in her family, and she had great quantities of carrot residue.

I said something in one of my books to the effect that if I grew enough carrots to make juice, then dug them, then washed them, then put them through a juicer, that I doubted if I would have enough energy left to hft a glass of the juice to my lips. And this woman was doing all of that for a family of 7! In a rather hazy fashion, I had assumed that juicing vegetables was done primarily for the aged, who

The Roman Vitruvius text De architectura libri decem, or The Ten Books on Architecture, is the oldest surviving garden design manual, dating from 27 B.C.

hadn't many teeth left. If one has his, what's hard about chewing a carrot? And what has happened to the idea of "roughage" which we've been told we need? But let's not be too hasty in our judgment; if we could drink all of our food, maybe we could entirely eliminate dentists.

Back to salad-making: When lettuce is ready to pick, there should also be dill, parsley, spinach to add, and lamb's-quarters, too, if there's any around. The tips of milkweed, also, and young radish leaves are good in salad, and perhaps tender beet and turnip tops, although I don't remember having tried either of these.

In my opinion every member of the cabbage family is good uncooked. You are of course familiar with coleslaw, and the others — broccoli, cauliflower (both purple and white), Brussels sprouts, kale, kohlrabi, collards — are just as good eaten raw.

I can happily skip raw beets and raw string beans, but I have never eaten very young ones. Fully mature uncooked peas taste a little bitter to me, but the ones which have been inadvertently picked when only half ready are incredibly sweet. The thing is to get settled in a comfortable chair for pea-shelling and do the job in a leisurely fashion, eating the young ones while you shell.

Corn, also, when it isn't fully mature, is very good raw. And as to the cooking of it, for my taste it is at its best when steamed just long enough to be sure that it is thoroughly hot. I think it is sweeter then, and perhaps the only point in cooking it at all is so that it will melt the butter that is put on it.

Summer squash is far better raw than cooked, in my opinion.

The biggest tomato fight in the world happens each year in the small Spanish town of Buñol. The festival called La Tomatina, involves some 40,000 people throwing 150,000 tomatoes at each other.

Pick it when it's still quite young and either add it to a salad or eat it with mayonnaise. Winter squash is also good raw but I prefer it cooked.

Any of the shell beans are good eating before they are cooked, and raw soybeans are really delicious, having a nutty flavor which the others seem to lack. The nutritionists are no doubt correct in claiming that soybeans have just about everything one could wish for in the way of a healthful food. If you have a vegetable garden I hope you plant some. Try the Giant Green variety; these stay green much longer than any other kind I know about and also are a good deal larger, which is important, because at its best the soybean is small and can be tedious to handle. It is hard to shell, too, but you can lick that by steaming it, pod and all, for a few minutes before shelling; the beans will then easily slip out. You can get Giant Green from Farmer Seed & Nursery Co., Faribault, Minn.

I have never been able to decide whether I like turnips better raw or cooked; either way they are wonderful, in my opinion. But I definitely prefer raw peppers to cooked ones, and this last winter I discovered something about the frozen ones. I always put a generous supply of peppers in the freezer, because I like them so much cooked with onions, and especially in egg foo young. By accident, I found that the frozen raw ones are almost as good as freshly-picked ones. The crisp ness is, of course, gone from the frozen ones, but they aren't mushy enough to be at all offensive.

And speaking of raw frozen vegetables, even the people who sell freezers will, oddly enough, tell you that you can't freeze toma-

Both George Washington and Thomas Jefferson grew cannabis on their plantations. Jefferson even invented a device for producing hemp in 1815.

toes. At least they used to say that, and when I mentioned this recently to a friend, she replied: "Well, there's no such thing as being able to buy frozen tomatoes."

By some odd lack of imagination, one apparently isn't supposed to freeze this popular vegetable simply because it can't be put into the freezer whole, then taken out firm and solid, ready to be sliced for a salad. We expect no other vegetable to retain its firmness and we don't abandon any other because it doesn't. Also, what about all the other ways of using tomatoes besides slicing them?

So if you go in a big way—as I do—for the flavor of a ripe tomato that has just been picked, gather some, wash them, put them in proper containers (cut the tomatoes up a little to save space) and freeze them. You'll find, when you eat them, that the flavor is intact, although the consistency will be closer to that of a cooked tomato. If you use the red cherry types they will still be fairly firm after freezing.

Being very careful not to exaggerate, I will bet that your own frozen tomatoes will have several million times more flavor than any you might buy in a store in winter or spring. And you have my permission to ignore everything else I have said in this article except the remarks about tomatoes. I do hope you will freeze some. They'll certainly brighten your menus in the winter months.

DON'T WORK SO HARD FOR ASPARAGUS!

There aren't very many of us who have more time, energy and money than we know what to do with. So I would like to tell you of

The word "radish' is from the Proto-Indo-European word *wrad, meaning "twig, root." First cultivated in China, radishes, along with onions and garlic were paid as "wages" to laborers who built the Ancient Egyptian Pyramids.

one way in which you can save all three, assuming, that is, that you want to grow asparagus.

The old-timers used to dig a trench two or three feet deep and a foot or two in width, then fill it almost to the top with dirt and manure, and put in the roots. Nowadays the authorities are backing down on this elaborate procedure, and are advising much shallower trenches.

Any reliable firm that sells asparagus roots will give you planting instructions. They tell you to dig a trench about a foot deep and ten inches wide, fill it almost to the top with very rich soil (if you can get manure, that's fine). If you must follow what they tell you about planting and making your first cutting and the length of time to cut each season. Beyond these things, my earnest desire is that you ignore the experts.

Some of them will tell you to plant a cover crop of soybeans and dig it in. This is unnecessary work. Others will say that manure should be spread over your bed every fall. Well, if you have some manure handy, which didn't cost you anything, go ahead and use it for this, but your bed doesn't need it.

Some gardeners put salt on their asparagus bed to keep out weeds, and I'm told that this is effective, but there's a better and simpler way to outwit weeds.

You may be told that you should cut the stalks in the fall, and some authorities even advise that these be taken off and burned. I suggest that you do neither of those things; just leave the stalks where they are. Like everything else, they will die when their time comes, so

In 2006, the average American farmer grew enough food for 144 other people. In 1940, the average farmer grew food for 19 other people (which was close to enough food).

let them rest in peace. They will help mulch the bed, too.

Let's just skip the fantastic idea of making mounds over the asparagus in order to bleach it. That's for the birds—and some Europeans, who were brought up on white asparagus and haven't seen the light. Nowadays, health-conscious people urge us to eat green-colored foods, the greener the better. Assuming that this is a beneficial thing to do, isn't it wonderful that for once the thing that's good for us is less work than that which isn't so good?

I've read that it's desirable to mulch an asparagus bed lightly in late autumn to protect the crowns, but we are also told to remove the covering in the spring and cultivate the soil. There is, however, no reason given as to why we should go to this trouble, and my guess is that the experts don't know why. It can't be to soften the soil, or to kill weeds, because under a proper mulch the earth is always soft and there aren't any weeds.

So what should you do? I imagine you will follow whatever method sounds most sensible and reasonable to you, and I wouldn't presume to advise you, but I'm going to tell you what results I get with my system.

I have two 50-foot rows of asparagus, one of which was planted more than 30 years ago in the old-fashioned way, before I knew better; that is, in a very deep, wide trench. The other was put in two years later, in a shallow trench. The two rows are doing equally well.

For the first 14 of my gardening years I covered my asparagus each fall with manure, cultivated it each spring, weeded it all summer

More than 100 agricultural crops in the U.S. are pollinated by bees. In fact, one out of three bites of food people eat is thanks to honeybees.

128

long. Then, one fine day in April (and I guess most of you know the story by now) I got the bright idea of abandoning plowing and hoeing and weeding. I covered my plot with hay, left it there, added more now and then, and for the past 26 years the work in my garden has consisted of replenishing the mulch here and there, and planting, and picking my wonderful produce.

This of course includes the asparagus bed, and, as I said above, I can't for the life of me figure out why anyone should think that the hay should be removed in the spring and the bed cultivated. The tips will come up right through the hay, so why disturb it?

It's true that mulch prevents the soil from warming up in the spring as rapidly as it would if the ground was bare, which means that your season will start a little later than it otherwise would, and also means, of course, that it lasts further into the summer.

For me all this is an advantage, because we get occasional frosts in May, and sometimes even in June; these kill any exposed asparagus stalks, so I'm glad to have the crop somewhat delayed. If, however, you are in a hurry for any reason—if, for instance, you sell asparagus and want it to mature early, when it brings top prices—it isn't much trouble to pull the mulch back and leave it off until the ground warms up, then return it.

Or you might push the mulch back on only a part of your bed, which would give you a longer season. You would in this way be cutting one section a week or two earlier than the rest, and you could cut the second section a week or so after you've stopped cutting the first. In general, leaves are a good mulch, but loose hay is the best for as-

According to the U.S Census, a farm is any establishment which produces and sells, or normally would have produced or sold, $1,000 or more of agricultural products during the year.

paragus; leaves, or hay that has been baled, may prevent the sprouts from coming through. Straw is all right. However, J. A. Eliot, of New Jersey, an asparagus expert, believes that hay is the best mulch of all; he says that for nutritive value it is superior to manure. And his reasoning is that part of the nutrients in hay, which is fed to horses and cows, go to build up the body of the animals, and to make milk; manure is the residue. But a rotting hay mulch still has all the nutrients left in it.

For the past 26 years I have used no fertilizer of any kind on any part of my garden except the rotting mulch and cottonseed meal. I broadcast the latter in the winter, at the rate of five pounds to every 100 square feet of my plot. I'm not really convinced that my soil needs the meal, but I have been told that it does, for nitrogen.

However, if gardeners weren't still driving in here quite often to inspect my system, I think I would skip the cottonseed meal for a season and see if it made any difference. But as long as I am exhibiting the excellent results which I get with my method, with so little work, I can't afford to have a failure. Who would believe it if I said the poor showing was only because I hadn't used the meal that year?

You can see, now, I guess, why I don't use salt to keep the weeds down. That's all that salt does, anyway, while mulch enriches the soil and does away with fertilizing. And it keeps the earth soft and moist.

Now a word about picking asparagus. People can't seem to get away from that slow business of cutting it with a sharp knife, or a two-pronged asparagus cutter, just below the surface of the ground.

Robert Newman was banned from all farms in the United Kingdom in August 2013 for having sex with a goat.

For my money, that method has four things wrong with it: it takes quite a lot of time; one is likely to injure a nearby shoot which doesn't yet show above the ground; the stalk-ends are dirty; and the tough part has to be cut off and disposed of.

My system is much simpler: I walk down the row and snap off any stalk which has matured, and since I break it where it's tender, there's nothing to be cut off afterward. And the stalks are so clean that all they need is a quick rinse under cold running water.

The amount of money my method of growing this vegetable will save you depends on how much you have to pay for hay, and how much you would spend for fertilizer if you grew asparagus the old-fashioned way. But I am sure my system will save you a tremendous amount of time and energy. As to results, a man who has grown and sold asparagus for 40 years, and who saw my bed, says that for such an old one, mine couldn't be better.

YEAR-ROUND VEGETABLES ARE EASY!

There may be areas in the U.S.A. where it's routine to gather — any day in the year — some vegetable or other from your garden. If this is true for you, please don't tell me. Who needs envious thoughts?

However, I have good news for those of you who live in less obliging sections, but are willing to go to a little trouble in order to pick something in your patch on each and every one of the 365 days. For the past year, I have been able to do this — from one to four veg-

Although only 2.4% of the world's cropland is planted with cotton, it accounts for 24% and 11% of the global sales of insecticide and pesticides, respectively.

etables (and many more, of course, in summer — even though my garden is in a frost pocket.) We practically always get a real frost around the middle of June, and one in early September.

During the years before I kept a year-round mulch on my garden, protecting the plants from frost was a major battle every season, and I didn't always win. I do now, though. It takes only a few minutes to toss hay, which is lying there handy, onto the plants. Also, I spread old blankets on raspberry bushes, and perhaps also on a wide bed such as onion plants or potatoes. In the fall I seldom try to save anything, although I may spread the blankets over a few tomato plants. Any green tomatoes I have left I give to a friend who makes a wonderful relish with them. The other tender crops, such as squash, peppers, beans and potatoes I pick and store or freeze.

So, with a frost in early September, how do I manage to have vegetables in my patch until the following March? Well, there are several things, as you no doubt know, that frost not only doesn't hurt but also actually improves. Cabbage, Brussels sprouts, turnips, kale, parsnips — all have a better flavor after being subjected to a frost. Or even subjected to several, butter- CRUNCH lettuce will stand a few frosts and so will new ZEALAND spinach. I don't know whether carrots would be improved or not by being frozen, for I have never let them "get it," I put bales of hay on them when frost threatens, then just tip over the bale and dig some when wanted. Last year, in early June, I served some raw carrots I had just dug to some friends for lunch, and they asked where I had found such good and so crisp carrots at that date.

In 2012, U.S. farms and ranches spent $329 billion to produce $388 billion in goods.

Now, which four vegetables can I get from my patch all winter? Well, carrots, as I have just said. Kale, about which I do nothing; this past winter the snow seemed to take care of it, keeping it fresh and green. I don't know how it would fare if there was no snow. After the turnips froze, I tossed on some hay, keeping them frozen. Parsnips are at their best—as you no doubt know—if left in the frozen ground all winter, then dug in the spring. I feel fairly sure that beets could be handled as I do carrots, but I like the former so much when cooked and put in the freezer in the fall, that I dispose of all I grow this way.

What can I bring in from my garden through March and April—up to asparagus-cutting time? Turnips and kale will have "had it" by now, but parsnips and carrots are available, and also—almost before you can believe it—dandelions and chives will be ready and waiting to be picked. I never seem to tire of those last two, served as a salad with French dressing.

Have you ever cooked potatoes (in their jackets, of course) and carrots, separately, then mashed them together and seasoned them with salt, pepper and butter? It's a very good dish. One of my kitchen bins is full of last year's potatoes, and under my kitchen table is a pleasant array of blue hubbard and buttercup squash.

The "authorities" say that kale may be sown in early spring for summer eating, but that some should also be planted in late June or July for winter use, the idea seeming to be that when planted in April or May, kale won't hold out through freezing weather. And I have more or less gone along with that, but last summer, for some reason

Out on a date and realize that you forgot gum or breath mints? Relax! Ask your waiter for some sliced cucumber with your meal. Take a slice and press it to the roof of your mouth with your tongue for 30 seconds to eliminate bad breath. The phytochemicals will kill the bacteria that are responsible for causing bad breath.

or other, the kale I sowed in July didn't mature. However, that which I had planted in early May was so plentiful I not only gave quite a lot away, but also had it available clear through the following February,

I discovered something this past winter about turnips. Although I knew they had a better flavor after being frozen, I had always thought they had to be cooked immediately after they were brought into the house. Well, I found that if you let them completely thaw out before you cook them, their taste seems to be improved.

Sometimes I wonder why I bother to freeze vegetables for winter use, since I would really be satisfied, during the cold weather, just to eat a Sweet Spanish onion sandwich each day, made with the soy bread mailed to me from Mease's bakery in Schoeneck, Pa. Incidentally, that bread is in many health food stores. It's flourless and delicious.

It really has occurred to me that it now is more or less a waste of time to stock my freezer with vegetables, since I seem to have figured out ways to have them available in my patch all through the year. However, since life is so unpredictable, the season that I decide not to freeze anything is sure to be the one in which each and everything I plant will decide to definitely "call it a day" around October.

FIND A WAY FOR STRAWBERRIES

One summer a friend said to me: You should see a psychiatrist about your abnormal affection for your strawberries—carefully tending next year's plants while your ripe raspberries, which you even

People in the U.K. call eggplants "aubergines". The word "aubergine" goes all the way back to the ancient Indian language Sanskrit. The eggplant is believed to have originated in India, where it is considered to be the King of Vegetables.

think are a better fruit, are crying to be picked."

He was right. But although I almost have a passion for growing strawberries, I can't figure out why they occupy such a special place in the fruit world.

For instance: it's February, you're expecting some company you want to impress, and you haven't time to make a cherry pie, or to attempt that elaborate recipe for Something-Or-Other-Supreme which you've never yet had the courage to tackle. So you buy a miserable, tasteless box of strawberries, (don't shop around; they're all terrible), wash and stem and chill the wretched things, and your guest will cry:

"Ah-h! Fresh strawberries!" And seem to enjoy them.

They certainly aren't much good, so why is this? Did it just get started, like the unreasoning and unreasonable hate and fear of non-poisonous snakes? Got started and kept on gathering momentum. Yet, with all this overbalanced enthusiasm for any old kind of strawberries, surprisingly few people grow them. Everyone says they're too much work.

And they are. Whether you put in a new bed each year or use two-or-three-year-old ones, you have quite a job on your hands. Transplanting is work, and even if you mulch to outwit the weeds you still have the fussy, time-consuming task of spacing and controlling the runners.

I started with Premier berries because someone gave me the plants and at that time I knew very little about the various kinds. Later, I was given some Fairfax and Catskill and discovered that Premier should be ashamed to show it's pretty but almost tasteless face

Horseradish is still planted and harvested mostly by hand. Sales of bottled horseradish began in 1860, making it one of the first convenience foods.

in the same garden with Fairfax. However, since we live in a cold Connecticut valley and Premier is almost frost-proof, I continued to grow some for shortcake, jam, and for the sort of people who like fresh strawberries in February.

Then one June, a friend who knows good berries, was coming to dinner. My Premier were ripe, Fairfax weren't, and as I opened some canned Fairfax (not frozen in those days), I was thinking that if I was that ashamed of Premier, I ought to stop growing them. And I did.

I now and then sold berries to friends and neighbors and got a top reputation in that hne which, however, wasn't hard to do as I had almost no competition.

After 25 years of experimenting. I've now settled (temporarily, at least) on Fairfax and Catskill. I have 70 feet of the former, 20 of the latter. I grow the Catskill because a season might come when Fairfax would go back on us completely, and although we snoot Cat skill as a dessert berry, I expect we'd unbend if we had no Fairfax.

For years I covered my plants with hay if frost threatened (we sometimes have it even in June), and how I hated to have to, time after time, cover those upstanding plants and drag the hay off in the morning.

I finally concluded that the cold nights stunted the berries even if they didn't actually freeze, so I stopped growing enough to sell some. But I couldn't bear to give up entirely; I loved to grow them so I asked my husband if he'd make some movable cold-frames for them. He made ten of these, 8 feet long, 3 feet wide. The lids are on

The name "kohlrabi" is made up of two German words: "kohl" meaning cabbage and "rube" meaning "turnip." The word "kohlrabi" literally translates to "cabbage turnip." This name is very appropriate as kohlrabi is a member of the cabbage family but has a large edible bulb that resembles a turnip

hinges and are opened and closed morning and night, so our frost problem, as far as berries are concerned, was solved.

At the same time, we defeated the birds, poor things. The frames are fitted with screens which are easily lifted in and out and are removed only when picking is going on.

However, frames or not, the work threatened to become a problem, come the time when I begin to totter from old age. I had solved that question for the rest of the garden by over-all mulching, but that, of course, didn't eliminate the transplanting of berry plants and spacing their runners, although it did outwit the weeds.

I'm inclined to really go along with the cliche "where there's a will, there's a way," and so it was with strawberries and me. You who would like to grow them but consider them too much work, might care to try the following system:

I planted three rows of berries, the rows about 8 inches apart. You can plant four rows if you like; I did only three, so that my frames wouldn't crowd the plants, which I put 3 feet apart in each row.

I let the first plant in each row make only one runner, straight down the row, and let the other plants in each row make two runners, one up, one down, the row. When I was finished I had three rows of plants, the rows 8 inches apart, the plants in each row 1 foot apart. But it looks like and is, actually, one row.

I planted mine in October, greatly preferring the fall season. A year from the following spring, after I had picked the first crop, I pulled up the first plant in each of the three rows, left plants number

The Greek philosopher Aristotle credited the clear voice of the partridge to a diet of leeks, while the Roman emperor Nero supposedly ate leeks everyday to make his voice stronger.

two and three, pulled up four, left five and six, and so on. In other words, I got rid of the mother plants and left the runners they had made. Then, during that summer, the plants I kept were allowed to make just enough runners to replace the ones I had pulled up. Year after year, the older plants are removed, the newer ones are left, and that isn't much of a job.

You have a permanent bed of strawberries and will never have to transplant again unless of course you want to try a new variety. You have to control the runners, but there is a tremendous difference in exactly placing only one or two runners from each plant and the old system of spacing a number of runners somewhat haphazardly.

If the bed is kept well-mulched, it will have no weeds. If you have a compost pile, you can give each new plant a handful of that earth, if you feel it's necessary.

Since I use neither compost nor manure, I let the ever-rotting mulch do the job. If I should ever feel they need it, I would give my plants some of the unbelievably rich dirt between my asparagus rows, which is composed of years of rotted mulch. In August when, I've been told, the plants make their buds for next year, I treat them to a little cotton-seed meal, for nitrogen.

I think my ground is now so rich from rotted mulch that I could get away with planting more closely and I'll probably try it one day.

One word about everbearers: phooey! But no, a few more: first, they won't produce for me, and second, the people I know who grow them have never, as far as I know, had enough to serve, although

Columbus evidently carried lettuce to the New World, for its culture was reported on Isabela Island (now called Crooked Island) in the Bahamas in 1494. Lettuce was doubtless among the first garden seeds sown in every European colony on this continent.

they may rush in from the patch with five, or maybe even six, berries in their hand, gloating: "Look, strawberries out of the patch at this time of year." If everbearers are a success commercially, why don't we see them in market in the autumn? I never do.

But what's the difference if fresh strawberries in winter are pretty awful and everbearers seemingly almost non-existent, if you can open your freezer and take out a container of last spring's delicious crop, looking forward to another June with its lovely gift of fresh Fairfax?

CHAPTER 5.

More Suggestions for Your Garden

THREE HOMEMADE GROWING TRICKS

When we bought our place here in Poverty Hollow, my mother had a cottage built near our house, and was in complete charge of the flower beds, in both our yard and hers. She placed them here and there—near both houses, against the barn, and had several

The health benefits of parsley include preventing halitosis, fighting skin cancer, fighting diabetes, promoting bone health, boosting immune system, serving as a natural antibiotic, keeping the heart healthy and detoxifying the body. Other benefits includes fighting arthritis, whitening skin and giving clearer complexion and promoting healthy hair.

on the lawn. Fred and my sister and I all liked this idea; that is, quite a number of small beds, with only one kind of flower, or perhaps two or three, in each bed.

But a professional gardener or two, and some other people who thought they were better informed, said that this was not only old-fashioned but also made a lot of extra work, for the grass was always creeping into the beds, which of course meant frequent clipping if the edges of the beds were to be kept neat-looking. Mother paid scant attention to these advisers, and we all backed her up because her arrangement of the beds was so attractive that none of us was willing to do away with these relatively small single flower beds in favor of two or three large ones with a lot of different flowers jumbled together.

And when I, much later, adopted the easy way of mulch gardening, it didn't do much in the way of solving the problem of keeping the flower-bed borders neat, although it did eliminate some of the clipping job.

Then, last summer, my sister came up with a good solution which is so simple that it seems absurd that one of us hadn't thought of it long ago. Here it is: All around the edge of the long, rather narrow bed of tulips (which could have, of course, been done to any shape of bed) we placed, on top of the grass, a thick border of newspapers, magazines, cardboard, and other like material, then entirely covered all this with some half-rotted hay.

The papers, etc., can be made whatever width you think best; just be sure that it is wide enough for the lawn mower to cut along

Sweet peas are one of relatively few plant species that can transform nitrogen from the atmosphere into a nitrogen form that plants can use as a fertilizer.

the border without getting too close to the flowers.

Now I cover the papers with dirt, and if the former are thick enough, it will be a few years, I should think, before they rot sufficiently for the grass to begin to get through. And it doesn't matter if there are weed seeds in the dirt; their roots are going to be thoroughly discouraged when they get down as far as the paper.

One could, of course, simply widen the flower bed, but there are two strikes against this. One is that the grass along the border will keep creeping into the bed, which it can't do under a thick layer of paper. The other is that few gardeners have enough willpower to refrain from planting in the wide border; then the lawn mower can't do the clipping. For this new trick you don't need self-control—just a lot of paper.

The second idea I want to talk about came to me a few years ago. I began to wonder (and asked John Lorenz and one or two other knowledgeable people) why some flowers and vegetables seeded themselves and others didn't. Was it because some seeds froze, while others were hardy? John said no, it wasn't that. Then our two great minds, working together, decided that, for one thing, most vegetables aren't left in the garden to make seeds. Dill will seed itself, and so, the second year, will parsley; gourds come up all over the place, usually where you don't want them. And I guess many of us find volunteer tomatoes here and there, although you won't see many if you mulch heavily.

I came to the conclusion that cabbage, for instance, doesn't seed itself only because it doesn't go to seed, and I thought it might

Unlike most veggies, cooking spinach intensifies the health benefits. Half a cup of cooked spinach will grant you threefold the nutrition as one cup of raw spinach. If you want to take it a step further, liquefying fresh spinach is the absolute best way to consume spinach – doing this releases beta-carotene stored in the leaves which enables your body to absorb the nutrients even easier than boiling it.

be interesting to help Nature out. I wrote Joseph Harris & Co., telling them of my project, and I ordered 9 different kinds of seeds. Then, late in October, choosing a spot in the vegetable garden, I planted the seeds, putting in beets, broccoli, early cabbage, carrots, dill, kohlrabi, lettuce, radishes, spinach.

You can see that I was conservative — planting no beans, corn, squash — in other words, nothing which took up a lot of room or would need to be babied along through innumerable frosts. My rough guess was that things might begin to germinate in, say, very late March or early April, and that would be far too soon to begin to try to keep a lot of things from freezing.

Well, one day near the end of February I went out to the vegetable garden with a friend to dig a few carrots. (I forgot to say that I had put an old metal cold frame in the garden and had planted the seeds in that, but don't get the wrong impression; I had left it open, and had used it only to give me a chance to protect the seedlings if, or when, they came up.) As we passed the frame, my friend asked: "What is that out here for?"

As I began to explain, I lifted one of the narrow boards which I had placed on each row of vegetables and saw, to my amazement, a very thick mass of tiny plants. So I, of course, went ahead and looked under every board; spinach, radishes, lettuce, cabbage and broccoli were up in greater quantity than I had ever seen. I suppose I planted them extra thickly, hoping that at least a few would survive.

But, I had left the boards on too long; the tiny plants were white and spindly. And another unfortunate circumstance was that

Virtually, the entire squash plant is edible. The leaves, tendrils, shoots, stems, flowers, seeds, and fruit can be eaten.
Presidents Washington and Jefferson both grew squashes in their gardens.

around this time I slipped on the ice and broke my wrist, and during the rather grim March which followed I didn't do anything about putting the top on the cold frame, or seeing to it that the plants didn't freeze. (My neighbors and friends were so kind to me, following my spill on the ice, that I felt I owed it to them not to go out and perhaps break a leg, also.)

A little of the spinach did survive, and a few carrots and beets showed up later and came through all right. I hope to try this experiment again next fall, and trust I will stay intact and be able to properly supervise the project.

My third trick has plenty: satisfaction, glamour, and if you are a person who likes to put it over on his enemies, it has that, too. I spent most of last summer (garden-wise) listening to sad tales from visitors about raccoons and/or squirrels getting their corn, and also fought to keep my own crop away from these marauders. Quite a few people told me that they weren't going to try to grow corn anymore, since it was mostly wasted effort.

In my latest book I blithely tell how to protect corn, giving 3 different ways to do this, the catch being that all of the methods eventually failed me. It must be that either these animals are smarter than any others, or perhaps they are like other corn-lovers (including me); that is, determined to figure out a way to win against all odds.

I did have a fence put up around my garden which keeps out rabbits and woodchucks—and which I fondly believed would also outwit the corn addicts, but it didn't. So, one winter, I told several men gardeners that I was planning to put up a corn cage (inside my

Surprisingly, Swiss chard did NOT originate in Switzerland. Swiss chard's place of origin is Sicily, Italy. Legend has it that a Swiss botanist was responsible for determining the scientific name and 'Swiss' stuck.

garden plot) about 20 by 30 feet and 7 or 8 feet high, with a wire roof on it. I could also, I decided, plant raspberry bushes in a section of it, thus defeating birds, for although I am fond of the latter (aren't we all?), I can love them a little more if they aren't feasting on some of my produce.

Each man I spoke to had a different idea about the corn cage, and I got more and more bewildered. Finally, I asked my brother Rex's advice, and he took complete charge — planning the whole thing, then ordering the material, then bringing his gardener and another man over here to help build it. They mixed concrete, put up steel poles, used turnbuckles (whatever they may be), and the finished contraption is really magnificent. If any raccoon can figure out how to get an ear of my corn now, I will admire his ingenuity so much that I won't begrudge it to him.

True, the cage cost quite a little (a few hundred dollars), but perhaps you could do the work yourself, thus doing away with at least some of the expense.

I guess you will agree that no one seems to approve of the way the other fellow spends his money, so when anyone says to me (obviously in criticism): "Did you really spend hundreds of dollars for that?" I in turn ask him a question: "Would you spend a few hundred dollars on a trip to Europe?" And when he usually says yes to that, I reply:
"Well, I wouldn't. But the cage is worth that much to me, for I can now grow corn the rest of my life without having to fight for every ear. And how pleasant it will be not to hate raccoons anymore! Al-

Female asparagus stalks are plumper than male stalks. It is the greener (or whiter) asparagus that are more tender, not the thin ones.

though they will, of course, all certainly loathe me."

PUTTING YOUR GARDEN TO BED FOR THE WINTER

Except for strawberries, putting the garden to bed is no job at all for the year-round mulcher. About all he need do is bid it good-night.

For those who haven't abandoned plowing for the over-all mulch system but are going to turn over a new leaf, autumn is the best time to start. Put all available dead leaves on your garden; toss cornstalks on them to keep from blowing. Then get plenty of hay — "spoiled" hay, good hay or salt hay.

Decide where your tomatoes will be next year and put corn stalks, cabbage roots, etc. over the area. (I cut corn stalks into foot-length pieces as I gather corn, making them less unwieldy). Now spread hay thickly over this refuse. When you plant tomatoes (late May or early June here in Connecticut) your ground will be soft, moist, and weedless. Don't be afraid of weed seeds; with a thick mulch they never get a break.

Cover your asparagus with eight inches of loose hay. Next spring it will come up through the mulch.

The rest of the garden should be more lightly mulched, be-cause next spring, instead of plowing, you will simply pull aside the hay and plant. Therefore, put on your heavy mulch after the seeds have sprouted.

This includes corn. You can save work next spring by marking

European sailors traveling to the New World used avocados as their form of butter.

the corn rows in the fall. Mark the rows with a firm stake at each end, leaving only an inch above the ground. If they are taller they may get broken. In the spring you need only rake back the mulch and plant. I give strawberries a light covering of hay after a few minor frosts, enough to protect the buds but not enough to smother the plants in case the weather gets warm again and they want to grow a little more. When the thermometer drops to 20 degrees I give the berries ten inches of mulch.

Now for flowers. In late October heap dirt (not mulch) around your roses. I use the unbelievably rich dirt from the vegetable garden, made from rotting mulch. This is better than cow manure, I believe, and is all the fertilizer my garden ever gets. I do nothing for climbing roses for the winter and they never show resentment at my seeming indifference. They bloom for me beautifully.

I never cut off peony tops. By spring they have died a natural death; in spring sometimes the dead tops have to be clipped off. I keep a constant mulch of dead leaves and their own tops around peonies.

And a constant mulch on the tulips. Quantities of dead leaves lie there all winter, with dead zinnias on them to keep them from blowing. The flower beds for annuals go to bed with a thick blanket of leaves.

So now all my garden falls off to sleep under a thick warm blanket. Natural, isn't it? How would you like to lie in bed on cold winter nights without a cover?

Native Americans flavored their baked beans with maple syrup and bear fat, and baked them in earthenware pots placed in a pit and covered with hot rocks. The Pilgrims most likely learned how to make baked beans from the Native Americans, substituting molasses and pork fat for the maple syrup and bear fat.

CHANGES FOR NEXT YEAR'S GARDEN

I have had a garden for more than 35 years. Wouldn't one suppose that it would be almost impossible to learn something new after all that experience? Well, it isn't.

For instance: One spring my sweet Spanish onion plants froze, a night or two after I planted them. Onions aren't supposed to freeze, but after disheartening incidents with peas, cabbage, sweet peas which I've lost from frost, I've learned to ignore what plants are supposed to do or not to do. But somehow it didn't occur to me that those onion plants were in any danger. That is a mistake I won't make again.

The catalogs haven't arrived yet, but I've a few thoughts about next year's garden anyway. One: No more rutabaga; for some reason it doesn't cooperate with me. Two: Even though Illini Chief ears of corn are tiny, and one is supposed to plant it 600 feet from other varieties (which I can't), I'll plant a row or two because it is so incredibly sweet. Three: I'll put in more perpetual spinach and Chinese cabbage than I did last season. They stand frost amazingly well, and we like them both raw and cooked.

Four: Late one summer Charley Wilson of Joseph Harris Co. came to visit me and he gave Rex and me each a packet of their new hybrid carrot, 318 Pioneer; I'll certainly put in some. Five: Last summer I decided to plant fewer peas; although we ate them almost every day for a month, I still froze more than I thought I'd be able to use. I was mistaken; now, in early December, I've already cooked more

One variety of banana, the 'Ice Cream Banana', is BLUE. It turns yellow like other bananas when ripe, and has a taste like vanilla custard and a marshmallow texture.

147

than half of them, so I'll plant four 30-foot rows again. Lincoln, of course. Six: I'll plant more yellow tomatoes next year. They are almost as sweet as pink ponderosa, which are so temperamental that one has to be a reckless gambler to put all one's money on them.

And seven: I hope I will do something that I've had in mind for a couple of years, but have not got around to, so far: order a package of asparagus seed, choose a spot somewhere in the meadow, and sow the seed on top of the grass. I want to do this because the finest, largest stalks of asparagus around are those hither and yon in the grass — self-sown, of course. With all the to-do about preparing a bed for this vegetable, the special treatment it's supposed to get, it will be inter esting if someday the experts find out the very best thing to do is toss some seed on some grass.

DO YOU SAVE SEEDS? WATCH IT!

I've been reading an article by Charles B. Wilson of the Joseph Harris Co. in Rochester, N.Y., which is called "How Vegetable and Flower Seeds Are Grown." I found it fascinating, for as the title says, it is about how seeds are grown, and I hope that what I quote here may be of some help to you, particularly if you like to save your own seeds — which, incidentally, I never do!

First, Mr. Wilson mentions beans, lettuce and spinach, whose seeds are easy enough to save and plant the following season. But he then calls your attention to cabbage, beets, carrots, celery and turnips and tells why we don't see these vegetables go to seed. It is because

Barley is one of the oldest domesticated grain crops. It has been cultivated for over 8000 years. In Athens barley was, according to Pliny, the special food of the gladiators (the hordearii, or 'barley-eaters').

they are biennials. That is, "they make a vegetative growth the first year, are stored over the winter, and not until they are set out in the field again the following spring will they produce blossoms and finally set seed." Mr. Wilson says that the cabbage plants make masses of little flowers which, "if all goes well," produce seeds which can be planted.

He does say that saving spinach and lettuce seeds for instance isn't as easy as it looks. "Under some conditions they may go to seed almost overnight but, unfortunately, when this happens, the seed may not have much vigor or the production of seed stalks may be so limited or irregular that harvesting is much more difficult." And he adds that favorable weather is necessary. As a matter of fact, "yields of less than ten percent of the expected results are not uncommon when the weather goes bad on you."

Mr. Wilson goes on to tell how careful a seedsman has to be in regard to distance between seed fields. Some varieties may cross when planted even more than a mile apart! That means, for one thing, that when one wants to grow several varieties of squash at once, he must plan with care. Well, when I read that, I got a little nervous about the two kinds of squash I like best —BUTTERCUP and BLUE HUBBARD—which run all over each other when growing in my garden. But when I read the next paragraph of Mr. Wilson's article and felt better, for it said: "Even though crosses between some varieties occur so readily, the home gardener need have no concern about them, since the effects of cross-pollination do not appear in the first season. It is only if the gardener saves his own seed, to plant the fol-

The Bartlett pears is named after Enoch Bartlett (1779-1860) who introduced it to America. It is also known by the name William's pear in Great Britain. Bartletts are one of the most widely grown varieties. Bartlett pear trees can still produce fruit after 100 years.

lowing year, that the results become apparent." (As I said before, I save no seeds.)

He goes on to say that, in spite of what many people believe, cucumbers won't cross with melons, nor will either of them cross with squash or pumpkin. And two different varieties of tomatoes rarely cross.

I think I'll tell of my experience in regard to planting corn. Actually, it wasn't a problem of crossing varieties, but of trying to grow a certain kind too near to other corn. In the catalog of the Farmer Seed and Nursery Co., of Faribault, Minn, (of whom, incidentally, I have a high opinion and from whom I buy soybean seeds because Joseph Harris doesn't handle them), I once noticed that they listed Illini chief corn, and that they spoke enthusiastically of how much sweeter it was than any other variety. So I ordered a package. And it was exactly what the Farmer Seed Co. said— incredibly sweet—that is, the first two ears that I picked were. However, the rest of that crop just sort of gave up; the ears were very small and almost taste less.

But I still kept hoping, and for two or three seasons I planted a few hills of the Illini chief corn at the end of each of my rows of other varieties. During that time, when Charles Wilson was here one day, I told him of my experiences with the Illini chief. He said that to get favorable results it should be planted quite a distance from any other variety; otherwise, it sort of reverted or something. And how far away? Well, the seed company now says, in speaking of this variety, that it should be grown "at least 600 feet from any other corn."

So, I regretfully have given up on Illini chief, for I don't think I

Dried bay leaves are used in Turkey and Italy to wrap licorice for shipping, and in China for packaging rice (to deter weevils).

have what it would take to start another garden across the meadow just for the sake of an extra sweet corn. Also, another cage (like the one my brother and Harold Salmon built for protection of my corn crop against animal raiders) would have to be put up for the Illini chief, otherwise, I can just picture what raccoons would do to corn as sweet as that!

The last half of Mr. Wilson's article is devoted to hybridization—and after a careful reading, I think I at last understand what goes on. He says that "A hybrid is essentially a first-generation cross between two related varieties. The result is a plant with greater vigor, which produces larger and more uniform fruit and yields more heavily."

He goes on to say that one of the plants used must be male, and the other female, so the plant-breeder has to see to it that the female plant is pollinated only by a plant of a different variety: the male. And to complicate things, many plants, such as tomatoes, combine male and female parts in the same blossom. Others, "like corn and cucumbers, have separate male and fe male parts, but both appear on the same plant."

In corn, the tassel is the male part of the plant and the silks are the female. Rows of each kind are planted in blocks, and as soon as tassels show up on the female rows, crews have to go through the field several times to remove them. Otherwise, some of the seed would be inbred instead of hybrid. All of which sounds like a lot of work.

Some flower species combine both male and female parts in

In 2009 North Dakota produced about 34% of the dry edible beans in the U.S.

one blossom, and Mr. Wilson says "To prevent the blossom from pollinating itself, the male part must be removed — a delicate task if the whole flower happens to be only a quarter inch or so in diameter." Pollen is taken from a male plant and applied to a blossom which is now wholly female. This is done to petunias, for instance, with a small camel's-hair brush or a pipe cleaner. "This explains, in part, why hybrid petunia seed is so much more expensive per ounce than even platinum." At the Harris Seed Farm, crews spend months in going from flower to flower as they open — cross-pollinating each one. And that piece of information makes me realize that if I hadn't given up planting petunia seeds each year, I would stop now; for, although my bed, which seeds itself, may not be as striking as the hybrid variety, at least no one has to go to all that work to produce the flowers.

To go back to the opening paragraph of Mr. Wilson's article, he says: "As you browse through the seed racks at the garden store, it is only natural that you should give little thought as to how the seeds in the package are produced. After all, there's nothing much to it; if you grow a row of beans in your backyard and let the pods dry on the vine and harvest the seeds, the chances are that you can grow a pretty good crop of beans from them next year."

Mr. Wilson doesn't suggest that buying seeds in a store may be somewhat risky. By that I mean (without any proven fact) that I have always felt quite sure stores keep their leftover seeds and sell them the following year, so you may find that store seeds don't germinate. Some years ago I decided to grow a certain variety of cantaloupe, and

The beetroot comes in 3 colors:
· Red beets are grown for eating,
· White beets are mostly grown for producing beet sugar and
· Yellow beets (manglewurzel) are grown for livestock feed.

for the first time it wasn't listed in the Harris catalog. I wrote and asked the firm if they had discontinued that kind. They said no, they hadn't, but that they had experienced a crop failure the previous season. They sent me a packet of that variety of cantaloupe, but wouldn't let me pay for the seeds because they weren't fresh and new. And under the circumstances, I accepted the packet with thanks.

(However, in my writings and in giving talks about gardening, I emphasize the fact that I pay for all seeds I get from Joseph Harris, for I don't want anyone to get the idea that the firm reimburses me in any way for the habit I have of often mentioning their reliability. Mr. Wilson once made me a present of a new variety of squash, making a point of the fact that it was a gift from him personally, and not from the firm.)

Well, I have got off the subject of Mr. Wilson's article, which ends with the following: "In trying to reduce the high cost of hand-pollination, the plant breeders have scored some successes, although most cross-pollination still must be done by hand. . . . Back at the turn of the century, nearly all of our flower seed was produced in Europe, but it is interesting to note that the first American commercial flower seed production of any importance was here in Monroe County (N.Y.) in the early 1900's. This was on the farms of the James Vick Seed Co., most of which has since been swallowed up by the suburbs. But one of the farms now belongs to the Harris Seed Co., and is still producing seed of vegetables and flowers."

Mr. Wilson has told me that many people object to hybrids, feeling they aren't "natural" — yet not realizing that everything that

The color of blood oranges is due to the pigment anthocyanin, not usually found in citrus fruit but common in other red fruits such as cherries and strawberries.

grows has innumerable hybrids in its genetic background, which are the result of crosses in the natural state. And he said; "It is fun to take visitors around and ask them to identify some of the crops they see growing. And when you tell them that the attractive shrub they are looking at is a cabbage plant, they find it hard to believe. Of course everyone can always spot Queen Anne's lace — only it turns out to be carrot tops!"

GIVE YOUR FIRST FROST THE COLD SHOULDER

Most gardeners are, I guess, more or less nervous when the first frost threatens in the fall. "Jack" didn't show up here until last night — about a month later than ever before in my 41 years of gardening, and when I went out to the patch this morning, I found over twenty reasons why I shouldn't have worried; if one has that many vegetables still on the job at this time of year, one could surely wait until next season for any that might have called it a day. (And, besides, my freezer is stocked with various ones.)

My tomato vines froze but the tomatoes, which are mostly ripe, are quite firm and as good as ever; I am over-supplied with them, but it's difficult to find any one who doesn't either grow them or isn't being supplied by someone else. We have enough potatoes to last all winter and they didn't freeze because they're under hay, but I'll bring all of them inside now. Peppers are the one thing I tossed a blanket on last night, so they're all right; in my opinion they taste better and are supposed to be more nutritious after they turn red, so I

The blue paint used to paint woodwork in Shaker houses was made from sage blossoms, indigo and blueberry skins, mixed in milk.

like to leave them on the plants until then; I've already gathered a number of red ones.

Usually I plant both bush and pole beans in good time, but this year I put the latter in so late that I thought they might not mature and I sort of forgot about them. But after that frost I took a look and saw that the vines were frozen but the beans, 'way up high on the fence, were all right and I picked the crop. Two rows of corn still have good ears on them, and New Zealand spinach and Buttercrunch lettuce are both holding their own.

A few weeks ago a friend of mine, (who is a very successful gardener,) asked me if I was eating dande- hons now, for, as you may know, young ones are showing up in many yards. I had been ignoring those around here, for we've such a variety of vegetables, but just a few minutes ago I saw several huge dandelion plants in the yard which I think I'm going to find hard to resist.

Do you grow collards? I made three different plant ings, several weeks apart, this past summer because I got the notion that they tasted better when young, but I think I was mistaken; we see no difference and since they are all right after many frosts, we are, like the tomatoes, over-supplied with collards. (Which we fortunately like a lot, though.)

My onion outlook couldn't be better — plenty for cooking all winter, and two bushels of Sweet Spanish which are so good raw, in a sandwich. There are, also, a lot of multiplying onions in my patch, which we can gather as we want them until the ground freezes, and then in Spring again, when it thaws. Do plant a few; one thing that

Borage leaves have been used to brew tea for hundreds of years. It was thought that when given to prospective husbands, it would give them the courage to propose.

will never desert you is multiplying onions.

There is still some kohlrabi out there, but it will freeze before most of the other cabbage-family does. The broccoli will last for a while and there are several good heads of both purple and white cauliflower, which also won't freeze for quite a spell and won't get too old in the sort of weather we can expect for the next few weeks. Do you grow the purple variety? It is very good and it seems to be more reliable (so to speak) than the white.

My Brussel sprouts are doing very well, and we can wait until after Thanksgiving—even to Christmas, maybe—before picking it. By the way, here's something about it which you may not know: Joseph Harris says, in his catalog: "About the middle of September, pinch out the growing points in the top of each plant. The sprouts on the upper part of the plant promptly start to develop more rapidly and attain larger size". (I have done this for several years and it works.)

Celery I don't grow, but we somehow feel that Chinese cabbage pinch-hits for celery. The cabbage is one vegetable that has to be thinned in order to properly mature, so we pull out and eat many of the first small plants, which makes thinning a pleasure; we either cook the young plants or use them in salad, but the matured Chinese cabbage has a large firm center and is wonderful eaten raw.

I plant both early and late cabbage and the latter can take a lot of frost. As to the early kind, I bought plants for about 40 years from a man in Bethel; when he retired, the ones I got elsewhere were unsatisfactory, so this past spring I decided to try to grow early cabbage (from seed) in Jiffy-7 Pellets. And I chose the Market Topper variety

Developed by Rudolph Boysen (1895-1950) in Anaheim, California about 1923, the boysenberry is believed to be a cross between a loganberry, red raspberry and blackberry.

because the Harris catalog said that it stood well without bursting. I planted the seeds on Feb. 26th and they flourished and I put them out in the garden on April 13th. And once more Harris was right; the heads stood nearly all summer without bursting. But the high point (if any!) to this cabbage story is that when I picked a head of it this summer, I didn't (for some reason, or, maybe, none) pull the root out of the ground as I usually do and, one after another, new small heads formed in the center of the old plants, and they're sitting out there now — firm and tempting. There are six heads in one of the plants and maybe you know that cabbage will do this, but it was news to me.

My parsnip plants look great, but we'll wait until late March or April to have that vegetable because of the good supply of others around here now. The parsley in the garden will be edible through October and November, then I'll take the two pots of it into the house; at present the pots are in holes in the ground and I keep the plants watered. And dill, which we eat raw about every day, couldn't have performed better than it did this season and is still going strong.

There are four vegetables which I can bring in from the garden all winter (unless I get snow-bound!), and one of them is kale, which, as you no doubt know, is supposed to have a better taste after frosts hit it; mine holds up in the patch until late spring. The other three are root-crops — carrots, beets, turnips — which can be left in your plot; I put bales of hay on them. And after tipping the bale over and gathering one of those vegetables, I have never yet forgotten to put the hay back; if you try this method, you better hadn't "forget to remember", either. Of course these crops could be put in your freezer, if you don't

The Broad Bean (Vicia faba) is a leguminous plant of the Pea family. Also known as: fava or faba bean, horse bean, windsor bean, pigeon bean, tick bean and field bean. It was the only bean known in Europe until the discovery of the New World.

relish the idea of going out to the garden in cold weather; I do that almost daily, to empty garbage.

I don't thin beets or carrots in the ordinary way; we pick very young ones — just big enough for a mouthful — and this of course thins the row. But it must be done carefully. As for turnips, which are supposed to be grown three or four inches apart, I don't thin them either, and I wish you could see mine now — huge ones lying up against each other. (There's no use in my telling how big they are; you would think I was putting you on.)

Just a word about frost and flowers: the portulaca in my yard, and the petunias, cosmos, phlox Drum- mondi, chrysanthemums, verbenas, didn't freeze last night and are, perhaps, at the moment, thumbing their pretty noses at the weather.

Broccoli rabe was originally cultivated in the southern Mediterranean. It was brought to the United States in the 1920's by Italian farmers. Broccoli rabe has been most popular in the Italian and Asian communities for the past several years.

CHAPTER 6.

Variations on the Year-Round Mulch System

Richard V. Clemence

ELEVEN WAYS TO MAKE MULCH WORK

Planting — Sweet corn, I have found, can readily be grown by merely pushing the seed kernels into the ground through the hay mulch. A string to mark the rows makes this kind of planting very quick and easy, and the yield is usually well above average.

Plant residues — After trying many ways of disposing of corn stalks, ranging from composting to chopping and spreading, I have arrived at a nearly ideal scheme. As soon as the corn is harvested, I flatten the stalks to the ground by bending them over and stamping on them. Then I cover the flattened mess with hay. In the spring, any

Brussels Sprouts were first grown in quantity around Brussels, Belgium, hence the name. They may have been been grown there as early as the 12th century, other sources say the first recorded description of Brussels sprouts dates to 1587 by Dutch botanist Rembertus Dodonaeus.

kind of plants can be set with a trowel through this cover. By spreading a little compost, loam or peat moss on top, even small seeds can be started, and the roots will penetrate into the decaying mass below. The results are astonishing to anyone who has not tried the method, and the work is reduced to almost nothing. I should add that I am not troubled with corn borers at all, and of course use no sprays or dusts of any kind.

Fall clean-up—My annual fall "clean-up" consists of leaving everything in the garden exactly where it is, and covering all crop residues with hay. I prefer to keep this cover fairly thin. If it is only four or five inches deep, it will be reduced close to ground level by spring, and seeds can be planted on and through it without moving it around. This not only saves work, but it also makes it possible to put rows very close together and get far more into the same space. Row spacing is mainly a question of the gardener's convenience. For most crops, I place the rows the same distance apart as the plants are to stand in the rows. Sweet corn spaced six inches each way will do just as well as it will with the rows three feet apart, and you get six times as much corn from the same area. Three rows of onion plants occupy a space only a foot wide, and so on with all the rest. Narrow paths separating crops of different sorts give you ready access.

Weeding—Hay is a marvelous substitute for thinning and weeding. Instead of pulling unwanted plants out of the ground, and disturbing the roots of others, I bend the weeds flat and pull hay over them.

Tilling—On most new ground, a few inches of hay in the fall

Those with thyroid problems should avoid eating large amounts of cabbage or cauliflower. They both interfere with the body's absorption of iodine, needed by the thyroid gland.

will make it possible to plant any kind of crop the following year without disturbing the sod. With the Stout System, spading, plowing and cultivating are all unnecessary, and do more harm than good. If a heavy hay cover is laid on even the toughest sod in the summer, plantings can be made through it the following spring. No other preparation of the soil is required.

Transplanting—Strawberries, tomatoes and other plants are incredibly easy to set through a thin hay mulch. With a string to mark the row, and a box or basket for the plants, you can move easily along, stabbing a trowel into the ground to make a deep slit. Shove the plant into this slit, step on the raised surface, and move on to the next. I can set 100 strawberry plants in a half hour without hurrying much. And they grow admirably, too.

Growing potatoes—Large crops of the highest quality potatoes can be grown by laying the seed (preferably small whole potatoes) on top of the remains of last year's mulch. I make double rows, fourteen inches apart, with the seed the same distance apart in the rows. The idea of this is not only to get a heavy yield, but to make it easy to inspect the vines from both sides occasionally, and take care of a rare potato bug or a bunch of eggs that the ladybugs have missed. Having laid the seed in straight rows with the aid of a string, I cover the rows with six or eight inches of hay, and do nothing more until several weeks later. After the blossoms fall, I begin moving the hay carefully to see how things are progressing. Small potatoes an inch or two in diameter can be separated from their stems without disturbing the parent plants, and the hay then replaced. What these small potatoes

What we call 'cantaloupe' in the U.S., is actually a muskmelon. The true cantaloupe is a European melon named after a castle's gardens in Italy. The cantaloupe was supposedly named for Cantalou, a former Papal garden near Rome, where the variety was developed.

taste like is something that no reader of this book should need to be told. The yield in pounds is reduced, of course, but the returns in satisfaction are maximized, Irish Cobblers are the best to eat this way, I think, but any variety with plenty of butter and home-grown parsley is a treat that few people have ever had.

Acidity Alkalinity — If you use hay mulch continuously for a number of years, you can practically forget all about acid or alkaline soil problems — along with dusting and spraying and the use of chemical fertilizers and "soil conditioners." I grow everything from beets to blueberries under the Stout System, and pay no attention to acidity or alkalinity any more. My experience has been that ample organic matter acts as an effective buffer and helps to neutralize extremes of pH in any soil.

Soil temperature — I have noted some discussion of the Stout System in journals other than this, and apparent difficulty in securing satisfactory results with it. I believe that the trouble has been due to a misunderstanding of the method. Piling a heavy hay mulch onto cold wet ground early in the spring is not a good way to begin using the system. Unless the soil is very sandy, or unless it is well supplied with humus, hay will give poor immediate results. Hay applied for the first time does little more than insulate the soil for several months, and if a beginning is being made in the spring, seeds should usually be well started before the mulch is spread. To improve germination and prevent washing, there is nothing better than a very thin sprinkling of peat moss over each row of seed. This light cover also serves to mark the rows, so hay can be spread in just the right places. If peat

Capers are the pickled, unopened flower buds of a Mediterranean bush and have been used as a seasoning and condiment since ancient Roman times.

moss is thus used, the mulch can be applied between the rows at any time after planting.

Garden boundary—I like to keep several extra bales of hay along the side of the garden. In the course of a year or two they break down into moist black humus, filled with earthworms that enter from below. Meanwhile, they smother grass that would otherwise continually be creeping into the edge of the garden.

Rotations—Perhaps my application of the Stout System to a rotation of strawberries, corn and potatoes would be of interest. These three crops all present special problems, because they ordinarily require so much space. For the backyard gardener to manage all of them is usually out of the question, and I have experimented for many years in an effort to solve the problem. The answer I have arrived at works very well, but it may be subject to further improvement.

Since this method is a rotation, we may begin at any stage of it, so let us start with the strawberries. I have eaten strawberries prepared in every way I could think of, and my notion of perfection is to pick the berries dead ripe after the sun has evaporated excess moisture, and eat them immediately when they are still warm, but swimming in heavy chilled cream. If you have not tried organically grown strawberries this way, you may still be wondering if they are worth the time and trouble they require.

Now for the rotation. I set a new bed every year, buying 100 virus-free plants, and spacing them in four rows one foot apart, with the plants also one foot apart in the rows. The plants are set through a

The carrot was brought to by colonists to the New World, where it escaped into the wild and became Queen Anne's Lace.

thin mulch left from the previous season, and more hay is added as growth occurs, and as weeds need to be smothered. Since I want results, not only on the strawberries, but on the corn to follow, I spread 100 pounds of Bovung and 50 pounds of bone meal over the bed as soon as the plants are well started. I remove all runners the first year, which sounds like a lot of work. Actually, however, it takes about ten minutes a week. A walk down each side of the bed, with a pair of grass shears in hand, will take care of the runners about as quickly as you would ordinarily inspect the plants anyway.

As early as possible the following spring, before the strawberry plants are getting into full leaf, I seed sweet corn between the rows and along each side of the bed. A string keeps the corn rows straight, and I push the kernels into the ground with my fingers, spacing them closely, and taking account of the way the strawberry plants are developing. When the berries are ready to pick in June, the corn should be four or five inches high, and easy to avoid in the harvesting. The corn should be an early and strong-growing variety. I have had the best luck with North Star and Golden Beauty, but others may be equally good. I count on the five 25-plant rows of corn to yield at least fifteen dozen fine ears, and have not been disappointed yet. While the corn is growing it needs no attention at all. The strawberry plants continue to live and to shade the corn roots, and the corn thrives on the extra Bovung and bone meal applied earlier.

After the corn has all been harvested, the stalks are simply flattened to the ground over the surviving strawberry plants and covered with several inches of hay. The following spring, potatoes are laid on

According to Mark Twain "Cauliflower is nothing but a cabbage with a college education."

top of whatever remains of all this, and mulched with a heavy hay blanket. Again, nothing remains to be done but to gather potatoes as they are wanted. According to the chemical school, everything should be riddled by insects and diseases, but I have barely enough evidence of these to realize what is supposed to be destroying my crops. I harvest all my potatoes with my bare hands, because it is so satisfying to handle the living soil and to discover one handsome tuber after another growing in it. The potato harvest thus leaves the whole space in perfect condition for the next crop. I merely cover the ground with hay, and wait for my strawberry plants to arrive.

I am convinced that the Stout System has great potentialities for the home gardener, at least, and that it can be readily adapted and modified to meet all sorts of special situations. I very much hope that these notes will encourage others to try variations on the Stout System.

MAKE YOUR GARDEN PAY

In one sense, of course, every organic vegetable garden more than pays for itself, since the money spent on it is returned several times over in the value of the superior food it produces, to say nothing of the pleasure of all the activities connected with it. In many localities, however, it is possible to make the garden pay for itself in cash, as well as in other ways. Where this can be done, all the usual advantages of gardening can be enjoyed free of charge. In other words, you can actually get paid to do what you would be happy to pay to do. All you need are a few near neighbors, and a little more

Celeriac (Apium graveolens var. rapaceum) is a variety of celery that is cultivated for it's knobby, globular root, which has a celery-like flavor. It is also known as celery knob, turnip rooted celery, celery root and 'céleri-rave' in French.

space than you use to grow vegetables for yourself. Your neighbors presumably buy vegetables, and there is no reason why they should not buy some from you, particularly since yours have a freshness and quality they cannot obtain elsewhere.

Now, as a result of extensive tests over a period of some years, I have concluded that ways of making the home garden pay are of two main types, and that the gardener will do well to choose one type or the other according to his own circumstances.

Briefly, the first type consists of doing the minimum of work, and concentrating on a single specialty crop of high value. The second type includes methods of production and sale that involve a good deal of time and effort. They are best suited to gardeners who have retired from other work and who find the extra activity more enjoyable than not. Let us consider these alternatives in more detail.

The gardener who is regularly employed in a business or profession, and who can harvest crops only in the evening and on weekends, can make his garden pay for itself by growing a specialty crop. The only real difficulty is in choosing the right crop to grow, and success depends almost entirely on your choice. Let us see what sort of product it should be.

It should be one that everyone particularly likes, so it can be sold without special effort. Your own favorite vegetable may not have such general appeal.

It should be easy to grow, with the minimum expenditure of time and labor. Crops that need thinning, weeding, or much other attention are unsatisfactory.

Using a celery stick to garnish a Bloody Mary originated in the 1960s at Chicago's Ambassador East Hotel. An unnamed celebrity got a Bloody Mary, but no swizzle stick. He grabbed a stalk of celery from the relish tray to stir his Bloody Mary and history was made.

It should be equally easy to harvest. Crops like peas and beans will not do at all. Strawberries, raspberries, or blueberries are not much better.

It should have high value for the space it occupies. Radishes, cucumbers, squashes, carrots, beets, and the like do not qualify.

The whole crop should be ready for sale over a short period. Since your time is limited, you want a specialty that can be marketed in a few evenings, or over a weekend.

The quality of the product should depend primarily on its freshness, so your potential customers will recognize that nothing equally good can be bought elsewhere.

Your specialty should be a crop that is not grown by every neighbor with a dozen square feet of land at his disposal. In some areas, for instance, nearly every one grows his own tomatoes, and though few may grow anything else, tomatoes would be the worst possible specialty there.

As you consider these criteria for a specialty crop, you may find it hard to think of anything that meets all of them adequately. If so, you are not alone. In many years of experience, I have found just one crop that is ideally suited to the purpose, and that is sweet corn. Fresh sweet corn is a delicacy that nearly everybody appreciates and one that comparatively few home gardeners grow.

Using some variation of the Stout System of hay mulching, in combination with close planting and manure or other organic fertilizer, an enormous crop of corn can be grown in a very small space. Virtually nothing has to be done to the crop between planting and

Pliny suggested that Roman General Lucullus introduced cherries to Europe around 74 B.C., but some research suggests that cherries were known in Italy at a much earlier date. Lucullus is said to have committed suicide when he realized he was running out of cherries.

harvesting, and the harvesting itself is extremely quick and easy. At prices of sixty to eighty cents a dozen, ten dollars' worth of sweet corn can be gathered and sold in an hour or two. In an area as small as twelve feet by twenty-five you can easily grow more than thirty dozen ears of corn, which should sell for at least twenty dollars. This is actually a low figure, I have always done better, and should expect any good gardener to.

Now for a few suggestions on production and sale. I assume that any interested reader already knows how to grow corn, or can easily find out, so I shall omit discussion of that.

If you live in an area that is not liable to late frosts in the spring, you will do best to concentrate your efforts on a single crop of corn, and to aim at having it ready to sell before any is available in the stores. In this way you will have a local monopoly at a time when demand is greatest, and you will be regarded as a public benefactor in selling it at premium prices.

If you cannot beat the market with your corn, it is well to grow two crops rather than one. Your early corn will thus be ready when your customers have had just enough of the store product to see how much better yours is, and you can inform all of them that you will have even finer corn for them a few weeks later.

A few telephone calls should locate all the customers you can handle. If possible, get them to come after their corn in person, and let them watch you harvest it. Customers who get their corn from you just before dinner, and cook it immediately, are going to come back for more. It will probably be the best they have ever eaten.

In the late 19th century, refrigerated railroad cars made salad vegetables more abundant, and available for most of the year. The salad fork originally featured curved claw-shaped tines and was known as a 'lettuce fork.' To provide leverage when cutting thick veins of lettuce or broad vegetables served in salad, the salad fork is made with an extrawide left tine that is sometimes grooved.

Husk all the corn as you harvest it, removing the silk cleanly, and snapping off any tips that are not filled out. This small trick takes very little time, and it enables you to see that every buyer gets perfect ears ready to cook. Explain to your customers that corn retains its flavor best if husked at once. This is not only good psychology, it also happens to be true.

Ask your customers what stage of maturity they prefer, and try to give them what they like best. Since you inspect all the ears, this is easy enough to do, and your buyers get corn that is virtually custom made.

Add an extra ear to each dozen without calling attention to the fact. Add two, if some of the ears are a trifle small. Customers who think your prices are high will change their minds when they discover this. Oddly enough, the extra corn is more appealing than a lower price would be.

Impress on everyone the importance of getting your corn to the table without delay. A customer who cannot do this should be told to get it into the refrigerator as soon as possible. Quality is what he is paying for, and he will appreciate your care in seeing that he gets it.

A gardener with time on his hands can use some of it to advantage by simply growing more of all his favorite crops, and keeping his neighbors supplied with a variety of vegetables throughout the season. He will have early peas for them in the spring, and Brussels sprouts after the autumn frosts. In between, he will have such delicacies as baby carrots and beets, leaf lettuce, scallions, early cabbage,

Garbanzo Beans or chickpeas are the most widely consumed legume in the world. Originating in the Middle East, they have a firm texture with a flavor somewhere between chestnuts and walnuts. Garbanzo beans are usually pale yellow in color. In India there are red, black, and brown chickpeas.

and vine-ripened melons. He will have at least one or two items to offer each day of a quality that cannot be matched by any store anywhere. How much money he makes naturally depends on the scale of the operation; it may be anywhere from twenty dollars to a hundred or more. Whatever the size of the enterprise, it should easily pay the whole money cost of the garden that helps to support it.

Although every gardener must develop his own program in the light of local conditions, experience suggests that a number of general principles are likely to be applicable everywhere;

It is better to supply all the vegetables required by a few neighbors than to supply only part of those needed by a large number. If you are able to count on a steady, if modest, demand for your products, you can arrange your plantings on an appropriate plan, instead of growing crops haphazardly and then trying to find buyers for them. By dealing steadily with the same customers, you learn their preferences and can satisfy them better as time goes on. You can also keep your customers informed concerning crops shortly to be ready, and they can tell you of their needs for the near future.

Remember that the most noticeable superiority of your vegetables over those available elsewhere is their freshness and prime condition, and be sure that your customers get the full benefit of this. Explain the importance of getting peas and sweet corn served within minutes of harvesting, and arrange in advance for delivery of such perishable items just before mealtime. Encourage buying for immediate needs, and discourage buying ahead for storage. Pass along hints on preparation and serving that will preserve the full flavor of your

The British and Americans speak the same language, usually, Then there are cookies and biscuits. And in this case, endive and chicory. What Americans call endive, the British call chicory, and what the Americans call chicory, the British call endive.

vegetables.

Keep your garden looking neat and attractive, and invite your customers to make some of their own selections on the spot. If they form the habit of calling in person for their vegetables, you can discuss the garden with them, and let them watch you at "work." When you are pulling a bunch of carrots for a customer, and he sees you casually discarding one or two with slight imperfections, he appreciates what he is getting better than he otherwise could.

Be sure that everything you sell looks as good as it really is. Since nearly all vegetables in the stores look much better than they are, this means that yours must present a specially attractive appearance. Every gardener knows that a slightly crooked carrot or a cracked cabbage is exactly as good to eat as any other, and it is tempting to convey this intelligence to a customer along with the item in question. It is better, however, to save such things for your own use. When you must supply something short of the handsomest specimens, make the price a little lower than usual. Be firm, but unostentatious about this, and it will leave fewer doubts about your standards than would any amount of conversation.

Do not be afraid to charge fair prices for your products. They are much superior to any available in chain stores or supermarkets, and they are likewise better than anything offered by roadside stands. It is the rare quality, rather than the cheapness of your vegetables that you should stress, and that your customers are going to recognize. If any of your neighbors is unable to see how much better your products are than those he can buy elsewhere, you do not want him for a

The seeds are NOT the hottest part of peppers. It is at the point where the seed is attached to the white membrane inside the pepper that the highest concentration of capsaicin (the compound giving peppers their pungent flavor) is found.

customer at all.

A good way to determine your prices is to check occasionally with the stores at which your customers trade, and charge the nearest price above this figure that is evenly divisible by five. In other words, if snap beans are twenty-seven cents a pound at the local stores, you charge thirty cents; if they are thirty-three cents, you charge thirty-five; and so on. This makes bookkeeping easy, saves trouble in making change, and keeps your prices in line with market conditions.

Keep accurate records of cash expenses and receipts. An excellent device for doing this is a low-price five-year diary in which you enter purchases and sales each day, together with any other data you wish. A useful technique is to keep totals up to date as you go, circling these figures, or distinguishing them from the rest in some other simple way. A five-year diary provides just the right amount of space for daily records, and has the special advantage of enabling you to compare the current year's operations with those of preceding years from day to day.

Do not undertake this method of making your garden pay for itself unless you are sure that you have ample time for it. If you are to supply one or more families with vegetables every day, you must be on hand to take orders and make deliveries whenever your customers choose to do business. To be sure, you can by prearrangement with them, take a day or two off from time to time. But unless you mean to be at home as a rule for other reasons, you should not try to keep your neighbors steadily supplied with vegetables. Another way of making your garden pay will work better for you.

Chives are believed to strengthen nails and teeth, and have antibiotic properties. It is said that chives are an appetite stimulant, relieve high blood pressure, and are a natural insect repellent. Chives inhibit mildew, and are used in feed for turkey hatchlings.

Although gardeners with limited time at their disposal are unlikely to be drawn into selling much besides their specialty crops, those who have plenty of time may be tempted to add the corn specialty to their other methods of making the garden pay. Since this effort can easily lead to trouble, it may be well to insert a word of warning here.

The difficulty in trying to combine the alternative ways of making your garden pay is that you must keep your markets separated, which is very hard to do. As soon as your numerous corn customers discover that you are supplying not only corn but all kinds of other vegetables to a few families steadily, they are going to want more than corn from you. If you refuse to sell them other vegetables, you are likely to lose valuable goodwill. On the other hand, if you try to sell what you can spare, these new customers are not going to be satisfied. At best, they will feel that they are getting what is left over after others have had their pick, and this will be perfectly true. At least, it had better be true. If you become sufficiently demoralized, you might try to please your new customers at the expense of the rest and make a mess of the whole thing.

My advice, then, is to choose the one alternative that fits your own situation, and make the most of it. If you do, I am sure you will find that making your garden pay its way financially is easy. You will also find that your garden is paying better than ever in enjoyment, quite part from the money you make.

Collard greens grow best in warm weather though they can withstand the cold temperatures of late autumn. Interestingly enough, the flavor of collard greens is enhanced by a light frost.

STARTING THE VEGETABLE GARDEN WITH LESS WORK

You can start a no-work, permanent-mulch vegetable garden "from scratch" in spring! There's no need to wait until your garden has been planted to spread mulch; you can seed and plant right on top of a heavy mulch.

My experiments were made on a small plot, 12 by 20 feet, where grass, weeds, and small bushes were allowed to grow until about the first of June. By that time, the growth was waist high and gave a depressing spectacle to anyone meaning to plant the area without doing a lot of hard work. The tests were as follows:

Potatoes—the small, whole Green Mountain variety—were placed on the ground, in rows roughly 14 inches apart, where they were completely hidden by the tall vegetation. This high growth was then flattened, and some six inches of hay spread over, leaving the seed potatoes at the bottom. After two weeks, the potato sprouts appeared, and grew into exceptionally large vines, yielding an excellent crop of fine potatoes.

Green Mountain potatoes are notoriously subject to insect and disease attacks, but these were troubled hardly at all. Potatoes, as is well known, thrive on potash, while requiring comparatively little nitrogen. The chemical "potato fertilizers" used by many commercial growers typically have formulas containing twice as much potash as nitrogen.

Now, rotting vegetation tends to lock up nitrogen, and a heavy hay mulch over weeds and grass would mean a nitrogen shortage for

"....while visions of sugarplums danced in their head". Those famous sugarplums which fill children's dreams at Christmas were originally sugar coated coriander, a treat that offered a sweet start and then a spicy burst of flavor. Later the recipe included small bits of fruit and became the confection we know today.

many crops. For potatoes, however, this is not a problem. Moreover, the same potash that can be recovered in wood ashes is released in the decay of any vegetation, so this scheme provides potatoes with plenty of that. (This is such a perfect way to grow potatoes that it is a shame I cannot claim credit for having originated it.)

Starting again with the same rugged growth of weeds, grass, and so on, I flattened it to the ground as before with hay mulch over it, but this time with nothing under it. I then dug through the cover with a shovel in a half-dozen places, and planted "hills" of squash, cucumbers, pumpkins, and melons. All these crops did very well, and were notably free from attacks by insects and disease.

The vines developed their fruit on the surface of the hay, where it remained clean, and dried quickly after rains. Hardly a weed grew anywhere in the whole area. The weed seeds near the surface of the ground had germinated and grown tall before they were smothered by the hay. Most of these were therefore gone for good. Other weed seeds still in the soil were not brought up by spading or plowing, so they did not germinate at all. The only foreign plants that showed up were four or five dandelions that pushed through the hay in mid season.

The third project was hardly an experiment, since it was an obvious procedure and certain to work. All it amounted to was setting tomato plants through the fresh mulch in the same way as through a mulch that had been longer in place. It involved moving the hay a little, and cutting through the vegetation under it to makes holes for the plants. I put dried cow manure and bone meal in the holes, and ran

The term 'corned' as in 'corned beef' refers to the very coarse salt originally used in the salt curing process. In British English 'corn' referred to any small grain or particle, especially those of cereal grains such as wheat.

the sprinkler for a few hours as soon as all the plants were set.

As you would expect, the results were all that could be desired, giving evidence that tomatoes may be readily grown in a new garden without turning the soil. This may not be astounding news, but I wonder how many have ever done it. It should work equally well with peppers and other plants, too.

Perhaps I should add that I have also tried setting the tomato plants in grass and weeds before applying the hay. This turned out to be considerably more work, particularly where the existing growth was heavy. With all the vegetation flattened under the mulch, nothing impedes the gardener's efforts.

The fourth experiment — growing other vegetables such as peas, beans, lettuce, etc. — began like the others with hay mulch laid over tall grass, weeds, and similar vegetation. In one test, I included cornstalks I had left standing for the purpose the year before. In another, I included strong raspberry canes spreading several feet from the main row.

In earlier trials, I had applied the hay very liberally. For the potatoes, this was desirable, and for the other crops it made no special difference. This time, however, I used only enough hay to cover the existing growth thoroughly, holding it flat, and excluding the light. Even so, the mulch was some three or four inches deep, and I used three bales of hay on the 12 by 20 foot area.

Before describing the rest of the experiment, I should like to insert a few remarks about the problems (and solutions) involved in planting seed right on top of a heavy mulch:

American and Canadian sailors on long voyages knew they could eat cranberries to protect themselves from scurvy -- making them a cranberry counterpart to British 'limeys.'

Seeds, particularly small ones, would vanish at once if placed on the hay, and would never be heard from again. The answer is to sprinkle peat moss on top of the hay along rows marked with a string, and drop the seeds on the moss. For the smallest seeds, a little loam could be mixed with the peat moss to close the spaces between coarse particles.

Seeds would tend to germinate slowly, if at all, on account of their distance above the moisture in the soil. This was an easy one, and running a sprinkler on the peat moss was the obvious answer.

Now for the procedures and results. In general, the planting procedure consisted of sprinkling peat moss, dried manure and loam (for the smallest seeds) along a wide row marked with stakes and string, scattering the seed, and pressing it into the prepared surface by walking slowly along the row. Rows were planted about 18 inches apart.

Peas. Two 20-foot rows of Lincoln peas were planted side by side in late June. One row was planted as I have indicated; the other was planted in the same way, but with the manure omitted. The row with manure grew strongly from the beginning, blossomed during a heat wave in mid-August, and bore a fine crop of peas. Not so heavy a crop, of course, as peas planted early in the spring, but fully up to the late crops I get by the usual methods. The row without manure started just as well as the other, but the plants soon turned light yellow, and later became brown and dry. Only two plants ever blossomed, and each of these bore one pod containing one pea.

Beans. Bush snap beans were comparable to peas as grown by

Contrary to popular belief, cranberries do not grow in water. A perennial plant, cranberries grow on low-running vines in sandy bogs and marshes. Because cranberries float, some bogs are flooded when the fruit is ready for harvesting.

this method. With manure, they seemed to do just as well as if they had been planted directly in good soil.

Beets and Radishes. As I suspected in advance, the method is not satisfactory with either beets or radishes, and I assume that it would not work any better with turnips or rutabagas. Germination and top growth are promising, but both radishes and beets develop long, thin roots that contrast most unfavorably with the globe-shaped specimens ordinarily grown.

Lettuce. Black-Seeded Simpson is the only variety of lettuce I have grown by this method. With manure it did very well, but it is a strong and rapid- growing variety that is hard to discourage anyway. Carrots. Since the main objective of the technique is to save time and labor, I think it should be regarded as successful with any crop that yields well, even if not quite so well as with conventional methods. On this criterion, the one test I have made with long- rooted carrots gave spectacular results.

I chose Tendersweet carrots for the experiment, and mixed a little loam with the peat moss and manure when planting them. They germinated very strongly, and grew so rapidly that thinning was necessary in about three weeks. The roots were unusually long and straight, smooth and well-shaped. On the basis of a single test it would be unsafe to attempt any generalizations, but it does seem possible that the method has special virtues in producing long-rooted carrots.

For everyone interested in this program, two points should be given special emphasis:

Bitterness in cucumbers can be caused by any stress on the plant such as high temperature, low moisture, low soil nutrients, etc. Bitterness is also associated with fruit harvested late in the season from poor yielding, un-healthy plants.

Adequate moisture is essential to satisfactory results. Unless nature is unusually co-operative, a plastic sprinkler or some good substitute must be made available. Ordinary soil tests for moisture are out of the question, but the hay mulch should be damp from just below the surface on down. This reproduces conditions in any good soil, encouraging the roots to continue their development. At the same time, it speeds the decay of the lower levels of vegetation, insuring that the roots will find their long journey worth the effort.

Keeping the mulch damp requires much less water than you might think. A first thorough soaking for quick germination, and a few more if rains are insufficient, will be enough. The hay cover dries from the top downward, so there is always more moisture in the lower layers than near the surface. If plants show no sign of wilting, irrigation is unnecessary.

Adequate moisture early in the game saves water in the end, for once the roots of your plants get well developed, they will find moisture enough in the lower levels during even a severe drought.

A liberal supply of a dried manure, compost, or some other complete organic fertilizer, is needed to feed the seedlings until their roots reach the soil. The commercial dried and shredded manure has, for once, an advantage over the real thing. Being virtually a powder, it readily penetrates down through the hay, and provides the best of nourishment for the plants as their roots develop.

SHOULD YOU GROW YOUR OWN SEEDS . . .

Is seed-growing a job for specialists? Or, can any home gar-

Cucumbers were brought to the Americas by Columbus.

dener increase his gardening pleasure by growing some of his own seeds? My answer to both questions is a strong yes. I know too little about flowers to offer any opinions about them. But as far as vegetables are concerned, I am convinced that, as a rule, the kitchen gardener as well as the man who makes a living from his crops should locate the commercial seedsman that suits him best and do all he can to make himself a steady and valued customer. What he will get in exchange is more than first-rate seeds. He will also get special attention to his orders, his share of scarce varieties, immediate replacement of seeds or plants that fail to meet high standards, and advice on his specific problems that he could hardly obtain elsewhere. Seed-growing nowadays is a specialty. And the best commercial seed specialists know more about seeds in a minute than you or I will probably discover in a lifetime. Furthermore, the code of ethics that prevails among the better seedsmen is nearly unique in the business world. If you display reasonable symptoms of honesty in your dealings with them, you will be met much more than half way, and your chances of being defrauded are nil.

If I recommend the seed specialists so highly, why do I also advocate seed-growing at home? In my experience, there are many good reasons for an organic gardener to grow some of his own seeds, and I will list two of the most important:

As most gardeners are aware, there are certain strains of recognized varieties of vegetables that seem to grow better and taste better than others. If you are fortunate enough to possess such a strain, you should perpetuate it, and improve it if you can.

The Coachella Valley in California is known as the Date Capital of the world.

This point is closely related to the first. All the best gardeners I know believe to some extent in the theory of acclimatization. That is, their experience, like mine, seems to show that the individual plants that do best in a given location produce seeds that also tend to do better than others, and that special strains may accordingly be developed for special conditions by seed selection. To the best of my knowledge, there is no rehable experimental evidence on this point. But in the absence of any to the contrary, I will argue in favor of it.

You will observe that either or both of these reasons could be challenged on strictly "scientific" grounds. So let me add this: If growing some of your own seeds can increase your gardening pleasure, that is the strongest possible argument for doing it. Given time enough, science may catch up with sentiment; but why wait? There are some material advantages to be had, too. Or, so I think you will discover if you have not already tried ideas like the following.

To begin with, you should avoid attempts to save seeds from biennials like beets, carrots, turnips, and most other root crops. Planted one season, they must remain in place through the winter to yield seeds the following summer. And the seeds must then be tested during a third year before results can be known. Darkness therefore surrounds such ventures for a long time. And when the light dawns at last, you are likely to find that the commercial seedsmen have been doing much better than you have.

The second thing to avoid, perhaps obviously, is any hybrid of whatever generation. I myself practice seed selection chiefly at the rock-bottom level, employing the "volunteer technique" I shall de-

Some call edamame the super or wonder vegetable because it is the only vegetable that contains all nine essential amino acids. This makes edamame a complete protein source, similar to meat or eggs. Edamame also contains isoflavonoids.

scribe shortly. And I keep all hybrids out of my main garden, for they can revert to fearful and wonderful things. A "summer squash" 3 feet long with pink and purple stripes hardly tempts the appetite, though it might be delicious if you could muster the courage to try it.

So much for what not to do. Now, what about a few positive recommendations? I have experimented with seeds a good deal over the years, and feel reasonably sure that real pleasure and profit in seed selection for most gardeners is to be had by following a few simple rules:

First, select an annual crop, like corn, beans, peas, lettuce, squash, tomatoes or potatoes, any one of which you are particularly fond.

Second, aim at developing a pure strain of your favorite variety that will be a genuine improvement on the products of purchased seed, at least under your own special conditions. Keep the strain pure by planting only the one variety each year where there is least chance of cross-pollination. Squashes seem to give the most trouble here, but that is only because most gardeners like to grow several different varieties at once. If you can arrange a location for your specialty a considerable distance from other varieties, you should do as well with squashes as with anything else. But unless you are prepared to develop a pure strain of any vegetable, you would better give up, for if you once get one kind mixed with another, you will never know what to expect from your seeds.

Third, choose your "seed-carriers" with special care. To improve your favorite vegetable, you must view each plant as a whole,

Eggplant isn't a particularly popular vegetable in the United States, but it's a favorite in many areas of the South. Thomas Jefferson, who experimented with many varieties of plants in his Virginia garden, is credited with introducing eggplant to North America.

and must not get confused by occasional fine specimens of fruit appearing among mostly inferior ones. It is not your best tomato or squash alone that you want to save for seed, but any passable specimens from the best plants you have. With corn or lettuce, the two factors are usually combined. But in seed selections, the seeds are the focus of attention, and you have to think in forms of the seeds you planted, what they produced, and how you can improve on that result.

The volunteer technique of seed selection is so closely allied with natural processes that nearly all readers of O. G. and F. must have had at least some experience of it. To be sure, there are still many "gardeners" who regard vegetable growing as a running battle against nature, and who therefore pursue such deplorable practices as "the annual fall clean-up," raking all organic matter from their garden areas, and leaving the ground naked all winter. But anyone who merely avoids these extreme measures is certain to discover a few plants already well started at regular seeding time, and to wonder whether he should encourage them to grow in the awkward places they have chosen, or whether he should treat them as weeds. As I have faced this question again and again over the years, it has slowly dawned on me that it is really a false problem, particularly for any gardener who has learned by experience that the more closely he can gear his operations to those of nature the better off he will be. So, what I have finally been led to is this:

As I harvest my crops, I keep two things in mind. First, the general plan of my next year's garden, and where the different seeds

The so called English walnut (Juglans regia) is native to eastern Europe and western Asia, and today the United States is the world's largest producer. English walnuts are excellent eaten as is; they can be candied or pickled, and are used in many sweet and savory dishes. They are also used to produce walnut oil.

will go. This may sound a bit difficult, but it is anything but that. I have a fence around my principal garden with posts just 8 feet apart, and I "rotate" my crops there by running rows in opposite directions in alternate years. Thus, with some years of experience behind me, I can see at a glance almost precisely where a row of any given crop is to be the next year. Earlier, however, I simply took a few minutes to think the matter over, and set a marked stake at each critical point.

The second thing I watch for is any unusually good plant — tomato, squash, pumpkin or potato — of which I can readily spare one or more fruit. I lay these in the garden litter toward one end of the row of the same variety that I mean to plant the next spring, and cover them with a few inches of hay. Actually, I make no special job of covering the seed-carriers as such. I merely leave them where I want them, and blanket the whole area with hay shortly afterward. When it comes to scientific seed improvement, this is about as close to nothing as anyone could do. But my Ponderosa tomatoes and Young's Beauty pumpkins started by this volunteer technique were so far ahead of my other crops as to give rise to comment from every-one who saw my garden.

Beyond the volunteer technique, which I doubtfully claim to have invented, I practice little seed selection myself, and recommend no more to others. After all, the professionals are really good, and you have to go some to beat them. There is one further practice, however, that I occasionally pursue, which is hardly more than a variation of the volunteer scheme, but which can enable you to eat your cake and have it, too. As I apply the technique, all it amounts to is a device for

Snails have been eaten as food since at least ancient Roman times. Apicius, the author of the oldest surviving cookbook (1st century B.C - 2 century A.D.) has a recipe for snails in his cookbook.

saving the seeds from plants I especially admire, and from which I have no seed-carriers to spare from the family table. The scheme involves slightly more work than the volunteer technique, but it has the compensating advantage of enabling you to eat your selected seed-carriers, both getting the nourishment from them and discovering if they taste as much better than others as they look.

I regard winter squashes as the ideal vegetable with which to apply this plan. When you harvest your crop in the fall, note the best vine you have, and store all its produce a little away from the rest. Then, if their flavor suits you, you merely save the seeds, air dry them, and store them in a dry place (warm or cool) until you are ready to plant them the following spring. For obvious reasons, this scheme cannot be used with lettuce or corn, and only with great difficulty with peas, beans or tomatoes. But with squashes there is much to be said for it, and with melons of any kind it should work equally well.

Cucumbers, of course, are a horse of another color, for they must be eaten green if at all, and the seeds of the big yellow specimens are the only ones that will grow. If you want to specialize in cucumbers, the thing to do is to let some of those on your best-looking vine get ripe and mellow while you eat the others. You can then gather the ripe specimens, wash the seeds from the pulp, and proceed as with squashes. Much the same is true of tomatoes. The vine-ripened fruit you eat falls rather short of the degree of ripeness suitable for seed preservation, and to get the best seeds from a tomato vine, the seed-bearing tomatoes should remain in place about as long

Farina usually refers to finely ground, purified 'middlings' produced in the milling of flour from wheat, but can also refer to a fine powder made from potatoes, or to other fine flours made from other grains, roots or even nuts.

as they will stay there.

As you can see, my notions of being a seed-grower are limited, and I am convinced that few kitchen gardeners can gain anything by trying to compete with the professionals on their own ground. Nevertheless, I believe that any ardent gardener can add a good deal to his pleasure by trying such modest devices for seed selection as I have suggested, and by developing his own special strains of a few favorite vegetables. In general, the commercial seedsmen have it all over us. But we do have one special advantage ourselves. We are working with our own particular soil and crops day by day, and we know which of our plants do best in our own circumstances. By making the most of this special knowledge, we can outdo the professionals as far as some of our favorite vegetables for our own gardens are concerned.

. . . AND ONION SETS?

Growing small onions from seed is easy enough to do. But in growing sets, the important thing is to keep the onions small until they are fully ripened. Otherwise, they will spoil very quickly in storage. Commercially grown onion sets are often produced on poor soil, so the question of excessive size is not relevant. Even so, many of the sets sold to amateur gardeners are large enough to go to seed instead of yielding good bulbs. Since onion sets are priced by the pound, the unscrupulous seller obviously does well to offer bulbs as large as the buyer will accept. Experienced growers insist on sets about the size of olives, and regard any much larger as rubbish.

Virtually all of the fennel plant is edible: the roots and stalks can be cooked and eaten as a vegetable; the stems chopped and added to salads; the bulb eaten raw or cooked; chopped leaves used in soups, with fish or added to salads; fennel seeds are used in pickles, liqueurs, tomato sauces and sausages; fennel oil is used in candy, liqueur and perfume.

To ripen small onions on rich soil it is necessary to grow them so close together that they cannot develop to anything like ordinary size. This means that the seed must be sown very thickly, not in a row, to in a "bed" where all the onions but those on the outside edges will be tightly crowded in all directions.

For an experiment, I chose White Sweet Spanish onions, and sowed a quarter ounce of seed over a rough circle some 3 feet in diameter. I decided to try Sweet Spanish onions partly because they are one of my favorite varieties and sets cannot be bought anywhere that I know of. Equally important, I regularly grow Sweet Spanish onions from plants started in the South. By planting any sets I could produce in the same rows with purchased plants, I should be able to get a useful comparison of results.

After scattering the onion seed, I sprinkled a thin covering of peat moss over the bed, pressed the moss and seed together against the soil with my feet, and watered the area thoroughly. I then, figuratively speaking, sat down to wait. In other words, apart from observing the progress of the plants from time to time, I did nothing about the onions at all. The seeds sprouted quickly, and the small leaves filled the space so completely as to make it resemble a plot of coarse grass. The bulbs formed nicely, and most of them developed to about the size of marbles by the time they were ripe. After the tops had fallen over on the majority of the plants, I pulled these, clipped all but a short piece of top from each with the grass shears, and chose 50 of the prettiest to store. They really were pretty, too. Round and white and gleaming, they looked and smelled delicious. In the interests of

Edible fiddleheads are the fiddleheads of the Ostrich Fern. Be careful, because there are many look-alikes (including the Bracken Fern and Royal Fern), which have been shown to cause stomach cancer in a relatively short time (2 to 5 years).

research, I ate 12 or 14 of them, and found them to be up to a high standard. In the further interests of research I managed to restrain myself from eating the 50 destined for storage as well, and put them into a small mesh bag I had provided for the purpose.

Up to this point, I had encountered no difficulties, and had not really expected to. Like most gardeners, I have grown onions from seed many times, and the thick planting was an obvious variation on ordinary procedures. Storage, however, was another matter. Onions keep best in a cool, dry place, and I might have found one for my sets. On the other hand, I wanted my experiment to show what might be accomplished by a beginner who was taking no pains whatsoever. I therefore selected a convenient spot in my cellar where it was hot and dry, rather than cool and dry, and hung the bag of sets from a nail overhead. As I realized when it was too late, what I should have done was to divide the sets, putting half in some cooler place, and leaving the rest where they were. I could then have said something definite about the effects of improper storage conditions in comparison with better methods. As it is, all I can say is that the heat did less harm than I expected. I did not touch the sets or even the bag they were in until late April, when I was ready to plant any that had survived.

I dumped the bag out onto the kitchen table, and sat down to examine the remains in comfort. Together with a certain amount of chaff, there proved to be 40 items that might be regarded as onion sets. On close scrutiny, a few of these turned out to be a little soft, and one or two more seemed unduly dry. Eliminating all but the very best, I had 30 prime sets out of the original 50, and these I planted at

In ancient Greece, figs were regarded with such esteem that laws were created forbidding the export of the best quality figs. Sycophant then derives from the Greek word meaning one who informs against another for exporting figs or for stealing the fruit of the sacred fig trees. Hence, the word came to mean a person who tries to win favor with flattery.

once.

My sets and the plants grown with them both ripened in late July. As far as I could see, there was no significant difference between the onions produced by the two methods. In rate of growth, size and days to maturity (90-100) there was no visible disparity. Indeed, if I had not carefully marked the area where the sets were placed among the plants, I could not have identified them later on. For flavor comparisons, I consulted an independent expert (my wife), who thoroughly tested both products in the raw state and agreed with me that they were indistinguishable from each other. From what I know of onions, I dare say this taste test was superfluous, but it was an enjoyable one to make in the interests of science as well as for more personal reasons.

I think that this experiment proves that it is possible, without taking great pains, to grow high-grade onion sets of a variety that cannot be purchased through regular channels. This question is the one that I was concerned to answer, and I believe that the results were conclusive. Obviously, however, I could not go much beyond this limited finding with the resources at my disposal. I should say, too, that I see no advantage in growing Sweet Spanish onions from sets other than a slight saving in money. Southern-grown plants give the same result for less time and effort.

SHOULD SEEDS BE TREATED BEFORE PLANTING?

Should seeds be treated before planting them? That is, will germination and growth be improved by giving your seeds some sort of

Common garden nasturtium (Tropaeolum majus) also called Indian Cress, Mexican Cress, Peru Cress and Jesuit's Cress, is native to Central and South America (not to be confused with the genus Nasturtium, which is Watercress). Nasturtiums are one of the most widely recognized edible flowers.

special therapy before placing them in contact with the soil? Since my experience in flower growing is extremely limited, it will be understood that I am speaking only of vegetables when I say that my answer to that question is very definitely No.

To begin with, I am sure that many other gardeners must be as annoyed as I am by the increasing difficulty of securing seeds that have not already been treated with some sort of chemicals. Corn, beans, and peas colored pink or purple grow no better than others in my garden, and they stain my hands and clothing extensively. What are these chemicals doing to my soil? I cannot imagine that they are improving it in any way by encouraging the development of the microorganisms on which its fertility so largely depends. Neither do I favor cutting seed potatoes, and soaking them in poison before planting them. Why not plant small potatoes whole instead?

So far, I believe that most experienced organic gardeners will agree with me. But beyond this, differences of opinion may arise, on 3 points in particular:

Lettuce is difficult to grow in hot weather, for the seeds will not germinate unless they are cool. Hence, some gardeners prepare lettuce seeds for planting in midsummer by cooking them in the refrigerator, or soaking them in cold water. This scheme works well, and the only reason I do not endorse it is that I have found it to be unnecessary and a waste of time.

Soaking almost any seeds in water will get them to germinate more quickly after they are planted. My objection to this practice is that, under ordinary conditions, you must soak the seeds as long in-

Spain and Italy were the first countries to adopt the fork as a utensil to be used at the table to eat with rather than just a serving utensil. This was in the 16th century. It would be a hundred years before the French decided to use the fork at table.

doors as they would take to germinate in place in moist soil. Surface planting is both quicker and easier.

The "inoculation" of beans, peas, and legumes in general with either a commercial preparation or soil in which such a crop has lately been successfully grown is a common practice, and in my opinion a superfluous one. If you are concerned about inoculation, just leave your old beans and pea vines in place, and give them a light blanket of hay or your own favorite mulch for the winter. Then, plant your legumes in the same spot the following spring, and inoculation will be automatic.

If your seed potatoes arrive when there is still snow on the ground, you can save time by spreading them out where the light will reach them, thus getting green sprouts started that will continue to grow after the potatoes are planted. The long white sprouts that form in the dark will not grow in the ground, so no time is gained by encouraging them to form. Sprouting potatoes is a simple treatment that I should favor if I had not discovered a better plan. I plant my own potatoes in the fall, covering them with 8 or 10 inches of hay or leaves. The seed is thus stored safely where it will not sprout until spring, and I get a nice crop for nearly nothing by using my own smallest whole potatoes for seed.

Since I have so little to say in favor of seed treatment, what do I advocate in place of it? Soil building, surface planting, and less blind faith in the virtues of crop rotation. On soil building, no competent organic gardener requires much advice from me. I prefer the Stout system of permanent hay mulching to other techniques for reasons

In the U.S. forks did not become popular until the 19th century, when the Rockefellers, Morgans and Carnegies popularized them.

that seem good to me. But the main thing is to concentrate on feeding your soil instead of trying to feed your plants, and to work with Nature instead of against it. All my gardening experience has convinced me that crop rotation, the adding of special supplements to the soil for particular crops, etc., are unnecessary in rich and living organic soil, and assume increasing importance as soil is poorer. As Ruth Stout has pointed out the secret of reducing your own contributions to plant growth is to let Nature do as much of the work as possible. The work, of course, gets done. But better than you could do it, and without cost to you.

Given a properly fed soil, surface planting of seeds will yield better results than any treatment I know of. Just mark your rows, push large seeds into the soil with your fingers and scatter small ones on the surface to be covered lightly with peat moss. Then run your sprinkler often enough to keep the seeds from drying out, and they will sprout very quickly if they are any good at all. Good crops of both lettuce and peas may be grown in hot weather by starting them in this way and applying a good mulch as soon as they are well up.

NEW WAYS TO PLANT VEGETABLE SEEDS

Seed-planting by the "usual" directions doesn't always work best. I've experimented and discovered some non-conformist methods that bring better germination, a faster start for young plants, and less trouble or risk for the gardener. What's more, these unconventional ideas add to the returns from a small vegetable plot — and subtract from the time and effort required to make sure of them.

All citrus fruits originated in the Old World, except grapefruit. Grapefruit originated sometime in the late 18th-century in the Caribbean. No one knows for sure, but it is probably a natural mutation of the pomelo and another citrus fruit.

How deeply, in fact, should seeds be planted? Have you ever given much thought to the question? If so, you may have been led to wonder why they should be placed underground at all. Seeds that are kept damp will sprout in the open air. Is the objective in planting merely to insure that the seeds stay moist? Or is it to get them down to the level at which their roots should develop? Or just what is the idea?

When I was a boy, it was already understood that peas would not grow well in hot weather. The reason was believed to be that the roots were affected by the heat, and growth thus retarded, an inference that has much to support it. The preventive measures, however, were another matter. In my youth, the approved practice was to dig a deep trench, place the seeds in the bottom of it, and after filling the excavation, wait for the peas to emerge. This outcome naturally took a long time. But the gardener was assured that the scheme would keep the roots of his peas far down in the cool earth, well protected from the sun's evil influence. Many thousands of cubic yards of soil were accordingly moved in the name of science, and many crops of peas were successfully grown despite the considerable handicap.

Most vegetables have astonishing powers of survival, and ingenious abuses are frequently mistaken for special secrets of success. So far as peas are concerned, few gardeners nowadays are unaware that the roots of the plants will penetrate just as deeply into the soil if the seeds are planted near the surface as they will if buried far underground. But how near the surface should peas be planted? Or other seeds for that matter?

The oldest cultivated grapevine in the country grows in North Carolina. The Mothervine in Manteo, Roanoke Island is a 400 year old Scuppernong vine. The Scuppernong or Muscadine grape is also the North Carolina state fruit.

Reflection suggests that there is a rather simple logic to planting. To begin with, the seeds are to be placed where the plants are wanted, which means in "hills" or rows. Next, the seeds need to be anchored somehow, to keep them from blowing away, and from being washed out by heavy rains. It is also important to place seeds in close contact with the soil, to keep them moist for quick sprouting, and to give the roots immediate encouragement as they start to grow. Are there other important considerations? Apparently not. A crop like potatoes is no exception, for potatoes are rarely grown from seed anyway.

Now, it would seem that the closer to the surface seeds can be decently planted, the sooner their sprouts will appear, and the more quickly the crop can be grown. This idea is consistent with natural processes, too. The seeds of wild plants fall on top of the ground, and though most of them may fall in uncongenial surroundings, those that happen to land in suitable places have no difficulty in germinating and sending their roots far into the earth. We are now approaching an odd conclusion: In contrast to conventional practice, logic would lead us to infer that seeds should be planted on top of the soil, and not under it at all.

I will admit that I arrived at this theoretical position some years ago, and that I was reluctant to prove it in practice. A few hesitant experiments were so promising, however, that I was encouraged to continue, and the results support the theory very strongly indeed.

I shortly discovered that my first successes were due to favorable weather conditions that cannot be relied upon once in a decade. Cloudy skies and occasional gentle rains will start seeds scattered on

Today the term 'grits' commonly refers to 'hominy grits,' but actually 'grits' is a term for any coarsly ground grain, like rice, oats, corn, etc. Hominy grits is coarsly ground corn (larger particles than corn meal).

the surface of the ground in an astonishingly short time. But high winds, a hot sun, or heavy rains will virtually insure failure. The problem, then, is to keep your seeds in place and moist until they germinate. After that, they develop as rapidly as their quick start would imply. The solution I have found after many tests may be subject to further improvement, but it certainly produces better and much faster results than do traditional methods.

To secure perfect germination in record time, all you need is some peat moss and a sprinkler. I recommend fine peat moss and a plastic "hose" sprinkler, but others may do almost as well. Coarse peat moss, however, tends to form a crust when exposed to the weather, and some sprinklers throw streams comparable to a water spout. With reasonably good equipment, you have only to do the following:

Mark a row with stakes and string over the exposed soil, and scatter your seeds on the surface.

Fill a large basket with peat moss, and walk down your row of seeds, shaking the moss onto them as you proceed, and employing your feet (preferably large) to step on the mixture of seeds and moss, pressing them firmly together. (A board or roller will also do the job.) Having reached the end of the row, you return by the same route, stepping on the spots you missed before, and leaving a perfectly planted crop behind you.

The function of the sprinkler is merely to guarantee results. The peat moss needs a good wetting to keep the seeds damp until they sprout, and rain may well be forthcoming at the proper mo-

Most of the herbs and spices that are commonly used in today's kitchens come from plants that were native to the tropical Far East, Eurasia and the Mediterranean. Red pepper is one of the few that originated in the New World.

ments. The sprinkler, however, removes all doubts.

As you can see, this system of surface planting eliminates rotting, blowing, and washing of seeds, and gets nearly every "viable" specimen started at once. No rain short of a cloudburst can move the seeds, for the peat moss absorbs water like a sponge. At the same time, the smallest sprouts reach the air and light immediately, and decay can hardly occur. Finally, sun and wind cannot dry or move your seeds, if you have a sprinkler ready for use. It might be added that the time and labor of planting are also reduced to a mini mum. In surface planting no furrows are made, of course, and the question thus arises as to how you get seeds like lettuce, carrots, and beets laid in single straight rows. The answer is that you don't. You don't even try to do so. On the contrary, you aim at spreading them over a space about a foot wide, using your marking string merely as a guide for one edge of the row. You thereby get many more plants into a given area than you can by other methods, and when you thin your crops, you save time and effort again. You can thin wide rows nearly as fast as narrow ones, and space your plants in both directions in one operation. After thinning carrots, for instance, you will have rows four or five carrots in width rather than one thin line of plants; and similarly with other crops.

I find that many gardeners shrink from the thought of rows more than one plant wide. They seem uncertain what is wrong about it, but they feel sure that something is. Perhaps the difficulty is that wide rows are not in accord with traditional practice. But, there is certainly no good reason why a plant should require more space from

Chicago got it's name from the American Indian word for the wild garlic that grew around Lake Michigan - "chicagaoua".

north to south than from east to west, or vice versa. It is hard to believe that many plants can tell one direction from the other. Narrow rows with wide aisles between them merely waste space in the home garden, without fulfilling any useful purpose. They have been copied from commercial practice which requires space for the operation of machinery. Broad alleyways in the kitchen garden are about as logical as six lanes of cement in the driveway. Such arrangements were designed for other situations.

Seeds like cucumber, melon, and squash may be surface-planted in "hills." As the word may suggest to some, though not to me, a "hill" is a shallow depression in the soil, an improvement on the genuine mound once used. The depression is usually made by filling a small excavation with compost or manure, spreading a little soil on top, and stepping on the area to press it down. In surface planting, you can prepare a hill in this way, or if your soil is rich enough, you can simply scatter some seeds in any convenient place. Then shake on peat moss, and press the moss and seeds well together against the soil. Again, the sprinkler provides insurance of quick results.

You can economize on your time and strength by scattering your seeds rather carelessly, and thinning hills to preserve only the most promising plants later on. If you conduct the thinning by clipping off unwanted plants, instead of pulling them out by the roots, you will not retard the growth of any of the specimens you choose to save.

Surface planting, as I have described it, has real advantages over more common methods. It can be used successfully with nearly

Today no-one in the British Royal Family eats garlic (so as not to have breath that might offend), and as a result no-one who works for them is a garlic-eater either.

all sorts of vegetable crops, and I know of only one important exception. In planting such crops as corn and pole beans, it saves trouble in the end to take pains enough to place the seeds in exactly the spots they should occupy, and to make sure that they stay there. The easiest way of doing this is to push each seed slightly into the soil with your fingers. Since they are not lying loose on the surface, peat moss is not needed to anchor them, and it is no better than any other good mulch for holding the moisture.

IDEAS FOR GROWING SWEET CORN

Sweet corn is—or should be—a gourmet's treat. The old saying that the water should be boiling before the corn is picked is only too true. It is simply impossible to enjoy this delicacy properly unless you eat it 20 minutes or so after it is removed from the stalk.

Yet too few of us grow sweet corn, and those who don't are missing one of the greatest rewards gardening can offer. The argument most often encountered is that corn requires too much space for small gardens in which every square foot must be productive. That is just not so, as a lot of us organic gardeners have repeatedly demonstrated in recent years.

In rich, organic soil you can space corn as tightly as 6 inches both ways and get excellent results. When I ran a series of experiments to determine if a small kitchen garden could be made to pay for itself, I found that tremendous crops of sweet corn could be grown in very limited areas.

Look at it this way. Sweet corn is often grown in rows of

Horseradish has nothing to do with horses and it is not a radish (it's a member of the mustard family). The bite and aroma of the horseradish root are almost absent until it is grated or ground. During this process, as the root cells are crushed, volatile oils known as isothiocyanate are released. Vinegar stops this reaction and stabilizes the flavor. For milder horseradish, vinegar is added immediately.

"hills" in which 4 or 5 plants are crowded together within a few square inches, while several feet are left between them to allow room for tractors with their attachments. There is no good reason why a home gardener should follow such practices. Even if you just have a narrow area 25 feet long and about a foot wide you can plant sweet corn 6 inches apart both ways and get 3 rows of corn with 48 stalks to the row.

That is very close planting, and unless your soil is rich, you may have to add manure, bone meal or another supplement for best results. But my experience has been that you can count on at least 10 dozen ears of corn from that much space, although some of the ears will be a little on the small side and a few stalks may bear no edible corn at all. Over-all, however, you are getting remarkable returns.

Furthermore, you can use the site for other crops at the same time. Pumpkins and winter squashes are the best I have tried. Planted along the edges, they start well and, after you cut your cornstalks, spread over the whole area. So, there is really no such thing as having too little room for sweet corn. I recommend wider spacing if you can afford it, but excellent crops can be had in small spaces, even outside your regular garden, in "blocks" here and there around the yard. In my experiments with corn, I several times grew more than 6 dozen just by pushing seeds through the mulch between my blueberry bushes along the front fence, and then waiting for results.

The best way I know to grow corn is in a permanent mulch. At planting time mark your rows with stakes and string, and push the seed through the mulch with your fingers. That may sound hke hard

Sixty two percent of all Idaho Potatoes are used to make processed products such as frozen and dehydrated; 29% are shipped fresh and 9% are grown for certified seed.

work, but it is really very easy to do on a small scale. For best results, open a small "pocket" in your mulch for each seed, and press the seed into the soil at the bottom. The objective is to create openings in your mulch for all your seeds, so they will sprout quickly in your best soil, and get the moisture, warmth and sunlight from the beginning.

My own preference is for the Ruth Stout system of permanent hay mulch. But I have also done well with leaves and other materials. If you grow corn as I do in the same area each year, returning all husks and stalks to the soil, it will soon be hard to say just what your mulch consists of. Some organic gardeners also report that a second feeding steps up or prevents slow down of corn growth.

After your small stalks get up above the level of your mulch, it is time to pay heed to their appearance. The thing to look for is color. In good organic soil, all corn plants should be dark green. And if they are, you have nothing to do to them but admire them while awaiting your harvest. A light green or yellow color, however, indicates a lack of nitrogen, and you should take immediate steps to supply more. But do not apply any chemical fertilizer! A deficiency of nitrogen at this early stage is a sure sign of poor soil. And if you simply add quick nitrogen, you will be in for more trouble later on. What your soil needs is an organic fertilizer like animal manure. You can hardly overdo such application on your corn. They will not "burn" it, and whatever is not absorbed by the current crop will enrich the soil for the following year. Once more, as you can see, I am assuming that you will go along with me on "crop rotation" at least to the extent of growing your corn in the same place for a few years. Try a few loca-

Juniper berries are the fruits of an evergreen bush found in northern Europe and America. Juniper berries are used in wines, beer, brandies, and is the key flavor ingredient in gin. The name 'juniper' derives from French 'genievre,' which is French for gin.

tions, choose the best, and then stay with it while you improve it.

Seed catalogs offer a bewildering number of varieties of sweet corn, and like most gardeners, I have tried a great many. In my best judgment, there is no such thing as a bad variety. Neither is there one that stands out as superior in all respects. Almost any variety grown in organic soil and eaten fresh from the stalk is a delicacy. Any handled otherwise is not. Between these extremes, choice of varieties is a question of personal preference—what will do best in your special circumstances? I have often eaten remarkably fine corn at the homes of gardening friends, only to learn that it was a variety that had never done well in my own garden. Similarly, I used to recommend my own favorites to others, who would frequently report that they thought little of them.

So, I am convinced that the right way to select varieties is to keep trying those that seem especially promising until you decide which suits you best. After that, concentrate chiefly on these while continuing to grow small blocks of newer varieties for comparison. In most seed catalogs, varieties are classified as early, mid-season and late. The earliest varieties are rather lower in quality than the others. But they have been developed mostly for their ability to grow well in cool weather, and taste astonishingly good until better can be had. If you are fond of sweet corn, you will want to grow at least two, and possibly three varieties to ensure a steady supply all summer and into the fall.

Contrary to common advice, I do not recommend planting all varieties at the same time. The earliest should go in as soon as danger

There is more to ketchup than just tomato ketchup. Some of the many varieties that have been popular include lobster, walnut, mushroom, cucumber, cranberry, oyster, lemon, grape, and anchovy.

from frost is past. But if the later are planted simultaneously, the seeds will sprout, and tenderer stalks will be exposed to cool weather they have not been bred to resist. The result is likely to be an unsatisfactory main crop, and a futile search for varieties that perform better under conditions to which they are not adapted. So, hold off on your later varieties until the soil has warmed up and the sun is getting higher in the sky. They will grow fast enough then to more than make up for their later start.

On the subject of varieties, I have a strong suggestion to offer as a result of experiments I have been running for the past 10 years. Choose an "open-pollinated" corn that appeals to you (I am using Golden Bantam), plant it in the same area every year; keep improving the soil by adding organic supplements plus all crop residues; and see if you can get a strain specially adapted to your conditions by selecting your own seed.

I cannot guarantee success, because the ears I was saving for seeds were eaten by raccoons last fall while still on the stalks, and progress was rudely interrupted. But Golden Bantam is a "dwarf" corn—and my stalks were standing 10 feet high, bearing ears a foot long when the raccoons moved in! If I had suspected that any was within many miles of my garden I could have prevented this catastrophe very easily. As matters stand, I am not prepared to offer convincing evidence on the question. But if you would like to try similar experiments, remember that hybrids will not breed true from your own seed, and that you must grow an open- pollinated variety to stand any chance of improving the breed.

Kiwifruit (Actinidia chinensis) were called Yangtao in China, their country of origin, renamed Chinese gooseberry when they were introduced to New Zealand in 1906, and finally named kiwi fruit when imported into the U.S. market in the early 1960s. The French call it souris végétales, 'vegetable mice'.

Besides raccoons, which are serious threats to few corn growers, the worst pests are crows, the European corn borer and the corn earworms. Let us take these in order.

Raccoons may be fenced out of the garden area with chicken wire stapled to posts that allow the wire to project a foot or so above them. Since raccoons climb fences rather than dig under them, they will find themselves caught as their weight brings the slack top over onto them. Any that manage to get beyond that point can be kept from doing serious damage by tying a paper or plastic bag over each ear of corn you want to insure, with a piece of wire screening over it. The wire prevents the coon from tearing the bag, while the bag prevents him from reaching the corn through the wire. The scheme is therefore virtually coon-proof, even if the fencing is omitted, though a pack of raccoons trying to get your corn can bend and break a good many stalks before they give up.

Crows, if in the vicinity, will pull small corn plants nearly as fast as they show above ground. What they are after is not the small leaves, but tender seed kernels below the plants. One solution is to plant untreated seeds through a permanent mulch that gives the plants a chance to get well started before the crows spot them. By that time, any plant pulled will yield disappointing results to the average crow, and after some communication among associates, the flock will move on to another stand.

The European corn borer and the corn earworm have little in common with the larger pests, but much in common with each other. Both are parasites that prefer their corn while it is still growing, and

Lemonade was a favorite of the Chinese Emperors. Lemons made their way to the United States with the help of Catholic Missionaries and were planted in Arizona and California.

both emerge from eggs laid by small flying creatures that look innocent enough as they go about their work.

Corn borers emerge from eggs laid at the blossom end of the stalks, and drill into the sweet cores just below the tassels. Once inside they eat their way downward until they reach the ears as large and hungry individuals, capable of ruining a crop very quickly. Earworms look like borers, but save a little time by hatching in the silk instead of near the tassel. Corn borers and earworms operating from opposite ends can really raise havoc with your corn.

Fortunately, neither is hard to control. Borers can easily be detected by casual inspection of any stand of corn and dealt with before they do serious damage. The holes they drill to get into the stalks cause the tassels to bend downward. So, in your home garden, all you have to do is to look for such evidence every few days and proceed accordingly. Split the stalk with your fingernails a little way below the entrance hole and remove the borer you will find there. That is all there is to it, and the simple scheme is virtually 100 percent effective. North of the Mason-Dixon line, shredding corn stalks by April 1st and covering them with soil effectively prevents the corn borer from laying his eggs in the stalks and infesting them. Some gardeners believe that widespread adaptation of this measure alone would soon eliminate the borer.

Direct control of earworms is equally simple. If you find one or more in the first corn you harvest, get a cheap oil can, fill it with clear mineral oil (you can get a bottle of it at any drugstore), and squirt a little onto the tips of your growing ears of corn.

The large, green, seedless limes found in your supermarket is the Persian or Tahiti Lime (Citrus latifolia) a hybrid developed in the early 20th century. The fruit is larger than the Key Lime, more resistant to disease and pests, and has a thicker rind. They are picked slightly immature, while they are still green in color (they turn yellow when fully ripe, and might be confused with lemons).

Although these methods are nearly fool proof, in the long run they are emergency measures and should not be needed. If you are troubled with borers and earworms you are not taking proper care of your soil. From my many experiments with sweet corn I am convinced that attacks by these pests are a sure sign of wrong treatment of the area in which the corn is growing. Several times, for instance, I have planted a block of corn in my best soil, and continued the rows into poorer ground. Borers and earworms have invariably attacked the undernourished plants, while leaving the rest strictly alone. Since all my experiments with other vegetables have revealed the same kind of thing, I am sure that rich organic soil is the answer to many common problems of plant pests and diseases.

I have tried to give you the best advice I can from about a half-century of experience in growing sweet corn. I have probably left out a good many things I should have said, and I can think of 4 pointers that did not seem to fit in earlier:

Never let corn stay in the husks after harvesting. Strip the ears, inspect them and return any to the soil that are short of perfection. If you have to hold corn for any length of time before cooking it, put freshly husked ears into the refrigerator.

Plant more corn than you want to harvest. Inferior ears and stalks are not wasted if they are used in soil building.

If you are short of space you can grow corn in small blocks nearly anywhere. You can run rows down a strawberry bed, in asparagus and so on. Single rows pollinate less well than blocks.

In returning stalks to the soil, either cut them at ground level

There are more than 18,000 different plants in the Legume or pea family (Leguminosae). Legumes are the 3rd largest family of flowering plants.

as you go and shred them with pruning shears, or pull them by the roots and chop them with a light axe all at once later on. Another possibility, and one I like on a good-sized stand, is to flatten the stalks to the ground and cover them with a hay blanket for the winter. This saves a great deal of time and effort and provides an excellent mulch to plant through the following spring.

GROW VEGETABLES ON YOUR FENCE

Every vegetable garden should have some sort of fence around it—not only to keep casual visitors from walking in uninvited, but more important, as support for growing crops. Take a small garden, say 20 by 25 feet, fence it with poultry netting 5 or 6 feet high, and you have increased your effective space by 50 per cent or more. You've also saved the time and trouble involved in providing stakes for tomatoes, poles for beans, and supports for peas.

As far as the fence itself is concerned, nearly any kind will do. The inside may easily be converted into a continuous trellis by fastening poultry netting to it. Or, you can run twine zig-zag up and down, looping it over small nails at top and bottom.

You can obviously plant all your pole beans, tall peas, and tomatoes close to the fence. Less obviously, you can plant many other crops along this ready-made trellis and count on their doing at least as well as they would if allowed to sprawl over dozens of square feet of your garden.

Cucumbers grow especially well on a fence. Instead of planting them in "hills," push a dozen seeds into the soil an inch or two from

Alexandre Dumas loved melons so much, he offered to the city council of Cavaillon all of his published works and future publications in exchange for "a life annuity of twelve melons per year."

the fence, about 3 inches apart. The vines will cover that section of fence completely, and you won't have the "curl" that often develops in cucumbers lying on the ground. You'll also find the fruit colors more uniformly, without the white streak that frequently spoils its appearance if not the taste.

Melons are another excellent crop for fence-growing. Watermelons, particularly the "icebox" varieties, need no other support. Muskmelons, though, should have "cradles" made for them out of cheesecloth, old sheeting, or similar material spread under the fruit and secured to the fence. Otherwise, as melons ripen and stems begin to loosen, the fruit will fall to the ground.

Like other vine crops, squashes and pumpkins will climb a fence as readily as they spread over the ground. If you have trouble with vine borers, however, it is better to let your vines run over the surface where you have had an earlier crop, and root them at the joints as they grow by covering these with soil. Butternut squashes, virtually immune to borers, may be grown on a fence in large quantities without difficulty.

In growing vegetables on a fence, remember that the principles of crop succession apply. Any given section of your fence can support more than one crop each season. Telephone peas or other tall-growing varieties may be started first. Pole Limas and Kentucky Wonders can go in a little later and a few inches farther from the fence. Tomato plants can be set a full root away, cucumbers, melons, pumpkins and squashes planted between them.

I am continually being told by people in cities and suburbs that

Mexican turnip another name for Jicama. It is the edible starchy, tuberous root of a South American vine of the legume (bean) family. It looks like a turnip, tastes like a cross between an apple and a water chestnut, and has a delightful crunchy texture.

they would hke to "grow a few tomatoes" or something of that sort, but have no room to do so. Over years of experimenting in vegetable growing, my answer has become: "If you have room for a fence, you have room for tomatoes—and many other crops too." So far, no one who has tried the scheme has reported anything other than success.

What I tell them amounts to this: If you want to grow tomatoes, get a dozen strong plants and set them within a foot of your fence in a sunny spot, if possible. Dig deep holes for the plants, and leave only the tips exposed above the paper "collars" you wrap around them to stop cutworms. Apply dried cow manure, bone meal, and similar organic fertilizers liberally over the surface, and wet them in with a steady fine stream from the sprinkler run gently for several days. As the plants take hold and start to grow, mulch them with hay, saw dust, a thin layer of peat moss, or grass clippings. When they begin to sprawl, prune main branches off to the best two or three, and tie these to the fence with strips of cloth, being careful to take a turn loosely around each stem with the tie made at the fence end. This gives you a "sling" for each branch which, like a surgical shng for a tender arm, supports it without risk of injury. After that, all you have to do is make similar slings for the higher growth, and you will have a nice crop of tomatoes. Let them ripen on the vines, and you'll have tomatoes far better than you can buy anywhere.

So much for tomatoes. The same applies to all the crops mentioned earlier, and possibly to others I haven't tested. Anyone who has a piece of fencing anywhere, or a place for one, has room for a good vegetable garden of corresponding dimensions. By feeding the

The common garden mint is spearmint, not peppermint as most people assume. Mint is said to be an effective mouse deterrent.

soil with organic fertilizers—including all crop residues —along a foot-wide strip next to a fence, you can grow astonishing quantities of choice vegetables at little cost beyond the price of seeds and plants.

POULTRY NETTING GIVES TOMATOES A LIFT

Tomato frames that support the vines at two levels, letting the plants grow through 30-inch-wide panels of poultry netting stretched between two rows of heavy posts, have never lost a tomato over the years for Leo Maurice, of Barre, Vermont. He reports that the highly effective and original frames cost about $5.

Leo's records prove that his frame has given him higher yields of tomatoes than other methods he has tried, and he thinks the wire mesh may yield some of the benefits of electrocuhure. The frame is designed to allow the plants to grow upward through two levels of wire mesh, spaced to cradle the untrimmed vines and fruit where their weights are heaviest.

His frame is erected on eight posts, set about two feet deep in two rows. The rows are 3 1/2 feet apart, and the posts are spaced seven feet apart in the rows. Crossbars nailed to the posts carry poultry netting laid flat at levels of 18 inches and 32 inches above the ground. In Leo's tests these levels have proved to correspond to those of the heaviest loads to be supported by the frame.

Tomato transplants are set as soon as the soil is warm in the spring, spaced about two feet apart both ways under the lower level of mesh. As the plants develop, they grew vertically upward through the mesh, setting fruit in largest quantities just above the wire supports. Since the plants are set about a foot inside the edges of the mesh on both sides, very little fruit hangs over the edges.

Leo has very rich organic soil throughout his garden, and he has found that his crops do better if grown in the same specially-chosen locations each year than when rotated. He therefore uses the same tomato frame year after year, and has substituted metal for wood in many parts of it. If a new frame is built annually, it should be made strong enough to support the several hundred pounds of vines and fruit it must carry.

AN ECONOMIST LOOKS AT THE STOUT SYSTEM

No system of gardening can be equally advantageous to all gardeners, and this is as true of the Stout System as of any other. Regarded as a method of production, any technique of gardening is a suitable subject for economic analysis. Let us apply such analysis to the Stout System and see what merits and limitations it reveals. In doing so, it must be understood that the facts to be analyzed, though true to the best of my present knowledge, may be different in the future, and may even be inaccurate now. To that extent, the conclusions would require modification.

Since the Stout System is a special type of organic gardening, it's obvious advantages over chemical techniques are those of natural gardening in general, and we need not list them here. An economic analysis requires a treatment of inputs and outputs in food production (I exclude flowers on grounds of my own ignorance) by the Stout

Mushrooms are commercially produced in virtually every state. Pennsylvania, however, still accounts for over 55% of total U.S. production. Abe Lincoln's mother supposedly died when the family dairy cow ate poisonous mushrooms and Mrs. Lincoln drank the milk.

System in particular as compared with organic methods of longer standing.

OUTPUTS

Inputs come before outputs historically, but we are considering them in the reverse order here in order to dispose of them quickly. Nothing in my experience of the Stout System, nor in that of any other gardener I know of, would tend to indicate that it regularly yields larger crops, or food of higher quality than other organic methods. We should note, moreover, that Ruth Stout herself has never made such a claim, despite the fact that many people seem to think she has. Visitors to her garden, however, know better, for directly across the road there is a larger organic operation than hers, comparing favorably in appearance with the gardens of Versailles, but growing food as well as ornamental vegetation. Indeed, the effect is so splendid as to distract attention from the state of the food crops. Close inspection of these, however, reveals that their condition and prospects are virtually identical with those of the same varieties half concealed by hay in Ruth's garden.

It might seem at this point that strict economic analysis has revealed no difference between the Stout System and more conventional organic methods on the side of outputs. That, however, is not so. Contrary to popular belief, the appearance of a garden is one of its outputs from the standpoint of economic science, and a Stout System garden is not beautiful except to Stout-System gardeners.

In a 14th century Italian cookbook there are as many recipes for mustard greens as those for any other vegetable, yet mustard greens are virtually unknown in Italy today.

INPUTS

In accordance with ancient economic tradition, we may group our inputs into the three categories: land, labor, and capital. Let us consider these in more convenient order:

Land, for our purposes, reduces to a site on which gardening is feasible. Since the Stout System is a type of organic gardening, it should be feasible wherever any such gardening is, and this I believe is true. I have known several gardeners who had difficulties at first in using the Stout System on heavy clay soil. Some resorted to spading forks almost immediately. But others found that the permanent mulch worked well after the first year, and increasingly so subsequently. We should note, however, that the old saying that the right time to start a garden is last year applies to the Stout System more strongly than to others, and that best results cannot be expected before the third year if the mulch is applied shortly before the first planting. Short of mulching a year in advance, the Stout System is best begun after the garden is well started in the usual way, and a summer mulch would be appropriate.

Land that is too rocky for regular tilling may be made into a good garden by the use of the Stout System; and the same is true of slopes so steep as to create serious problems of erosion and washout unless terracing is undertaken,

Capital in the form of tools and equipment appears to reduce to little more than a hoe and pitchfork in the Stout System in contrast to substantially greater requirements of other methods. Experienced gardeners will realize, however, that the real minimum capital re-

"Working in the garden gives me something beyond the enjoyment of the senses. It gives me a profound feeling of inner peace."

— Ruth Stout

quirement for any kind of organic gardening is zero, and that all the work can, if necessary, be done with the bare hands. Above the zero level, capital tends to vary roughly with the size of the garden but the controlling factors, as we all know, are actually the tastes and interests of the gardener. Very few of us have failed to acquire over the years a substantial inventory of gadgets that we rarely, if ever, use. And many of us go in for power machinery far beyond our genuine needs. The fact is that nearly all gardeners enjoy the possession and use of good capital equipment. It can add a great deal to the pleasure of gardening; and to the extent that it does, it is economically sound.

It may, I think, rightly be said of the Stout System that it affords rather less temptation to splurge on capital equipment than do other methods. How important an advantage this is depends on the individual gardener.

Labor, in the form of the time and energy of the gardener, is the most important type of input for most of us. As the titles of Ruth Stout's "How To Have A Green Thumb Without An Aching Back" and "Gardening Without Work" imply, the principal advantage claimed for the Stout System relates to this labor input. The permanent mulch, consisting largely of hay, is maintained with little more labor than is required for ordinary summer mulching. But in addition to the weed control, moisture preservation and other merits of summer mulch, the Stout System once established, transfers the work of tilling, hoeing, cultivating and fertilizing from the gardener to natural processes. This fact alone may be sufficient to commend the method to those who wish to garden with nature as closely as possible. For

"There is peace in the garden. Peace and results."

— Ruth Stout

them, our economic analysis ends here, since we already know the right decision for these gardeners. For others, however, there is more to be done.

SUMMARY OF RESULTS

Before completing our economic analysis it may be well to summarize the main points on which our conclusions depend.

On the output side, the Stout System has no considerable advantage over other types of organic gardening. Indeed, gardeners who attach high value to a parklike appearance will find the Stout System inferior in terms of esthetic returns.

On the input side, the Stout System has some slight advantage in land and virtually none in capital. By far its most striking advantage is in labor, defined as a combination of time and intensity of effort.

To see how the importance of labor inputs to the gardener is determined, we must apply the economic principle of opportunity cost. According to this principle, the true cost of doing anything is the best alter native opportunity that must be given up. Thus, the real cost to the reader of reading these words is the best use he could otherwise make of his time and energy. I am aware of the fact that my use of this example may lose me some readers at this point by reminding them that they have better things to do. This hazard however, serves to emphasize the point that only the person most concerned (in our case the gardener) can accurately determine the real cost of anything to himself (here, labor inputs) by his own due

Navy Beans are small, white and oval with a refined texture and delicate flavor. These are the beans used for the famous Boston and English baked beans. Because their skin and fine texture do not break up on cooking. These beans were named for their part of the U.S. Navy diet during the second half of the 19th Century.

thought.

CONCLUSIONS

No economist can determine the real cost of labor inputs to anyone but himself. Logically, however, the cost of each of these inputs to everyone must vary inversely with the number at his disposal. Thus, gardeners with the least time and energy at their disposal must attach a higher value to each hour than those with more. Applying this economic principle to the Stout System will enable us to make a rough classification of gardeners in order of probable appeal.

In our first group we may place those gardeners and would-be gardeners to whom labor inputs have the highest value. The sub-title of "Gardening Without Work" is "For the Aging, the Busy, and the Indolent;" and that covers most of the relevant ground. There are many potential gardeners who are unable or unwilling to take labor inputs enough from other uses to garden by other methods. For them it is the Stout System or nothing.

People with more time and energy to spare will place less value on their labor inputs, and may therefore be influenced more by appearance of their gardens and similar factors than those in the first group. The larger their gardens the more likely they will be to favor the Stout System or some combination of it and other methods; for their available labor inputs are, after all, limited.

To the young, idle, and the energetic, labor inputs have least value, and except on very large areas the Stout System will appeal least to them. Since I am aging and busy, and perhaps even indolent,

Peach seeds may occasionally grow into trees that bear nectarines, and nectarine seeds may grow into trees that bear either nectarines or peaches. It is not possible to know which fruit will grow on trees grown from nectarine seeds, so nectarine branches are grafted onto peach trees to guarantee a crop of nectarines.

to say nothing of being a professional economist, I allocate my own labor inputs with a strict view to maximum returns from all uses. I am aware, however, that there are large numbers of otherwise rational people to whom physical labor is a pleasure in itself. They would actually prefer to terrace a steep slope that might readily have been gardened by the Stout System.

Altogether, we may conclude that economic analysis shows the Stout System to be of limited appeal to some types of gardeners and of strong appeal to others. Which type is more numerous can be determined only as "no-work" techniques become more widely known. Meanwhile, we may safely say that its greatest value lies in bringing organic gardening within the reach of a large class of potential gardeners who would otherwise not garden at all.

Richard V. Clemence

"It's a fair-sized job to write a book that people can be bothered just to read; when they begin to steal copies, you are really getting some place."

— Ruth Stout

The End.

"The unmulched garden looks to me like some naked thing which for one reason or another would be better off with a few clothes on."

— *Ruth Stout*

"If you have the soul of a gardener, not for anything would you work with gloves on."

— *Ruth Stout*

Nicknamed the "Mulch Queen", Ruth Stout was born in the United States in 1884. As early as 1920, she realized that all traditional methods of working with the soil (digging, weeding, watering, plowing, hoeing), could be replaced by simply adding a layer of hay on the ground. She wrote a chronicle about this particular approach for the magazine Organic Farming and Gardening from 1953 to 1971. She also published several books about her methods. Stout emphasized the simplicity of her methods, and the way the gardener benefits from extra free time and rest. It's easy to see with the titles of her books: Gardening Without Work, I've Always Done It My Way, and How to Have a Green Thumb Without an Aching Back . In light of the fascinating results she obtained in her gardens, she didn't shy away from challenging traditional methods of gardening. She made it a principle to speak only from experience, only from the results she had observed herself.

www.MulchQueen.com

MEET THE PUBLISHER

12 Sirens was founded by a group of firefighters to showcase a array of media ranging from culinary to nautical to self-improvement. With locations in Seattle, the Deep South and Europe, 12 Sirens looks to shine a spotlight on the unusual that still generates interest and value.

www.12Sirens.com

9 781927 458365